Samuel Zane Batten

The New Citizenship

Christian character in its Biblical ideals, sources, and relations

Samuel Zane Batten

The New Citizenship
Christian character in its Biblical ideals, sources, and relations

ISBN/EAN: 9783337037680

Printed in Europe, USA, Canada, Australia, Japan

Cover: Foto ©Lupo / pixelio.de

More available books at **www.hansebooks.com**

[Green Fund Book, No. 12 a.]

THE NEW CITIZENSHIP

CHRISTIAN CHARACTER IN ITS BIBLICAL
IDEALS, SOURCES, AND RELATIONS

BY
SAMUEL ZANE BATTEN

"See that thou make all things according to the pattern shewed to thee in the mount."

ANALYSIS OF CONTENTS.

INTRODUCTORY: WHENCE AND WHITHER.

	PAGE.
The glory of Christianity is its manifoldness...	6
Its vitality shown in different ideals of character...	7
1. The first three centuries of Christianity..	8
2. The ascetic ideal..........	9–11
3. The church devotee..........	12
4. The Reformation and liberty..........	13
These ideals more or less blended and interfused..........	14
5. The new ideal..........	15
The sense of humanity-solidarity....	16–17
Bunyan's Pilgrim—The New Pilgrim.	18
Progress in character measured.....	19
The breadth of salvation..........	20
Mistaken conceptions of Christian character and sainthood..........	
Jesus Christ in the world..........	22
Christianity an earth religion........	23
The sainthood of everyday life.....	24
Character gained and maintained...	25
Thesis: Learning the New Citizenship in the kingdom of God is to develop right..	
Christian character................	27

Two things emphasized:

1. Growth of character fulfilling relationships..........	27
2. Character to be formed in everyday world..........	28

1

ANALYSIS OF CONTENTS.

CHAPTER I. VISIONS AND IDEALS.

	PAGE
Right thought goes before right action	29
I. The Necessity of Right Ideals	30
Ruskin's two pictures	30–32
Justified by vision	32
Two kinds of men	33
Great ideas cause great achievements	34–35
II. The Ideals that are to be Cherished	
1. Ideals of the worth of life	37
Life a vanity	37
Life a great thing	39
2. Ideals of Truth	
What is truth?	39–40
Truth pole star	40
3. Ideals of progress	
Despairing views of world	41
World not exhausted	42
III. The Transforming Power of a Right Ideal	43
Two girls and two pictures	43–44
Image of God, why forbidden	45
Transformed by beholding	46
Till Christ be formed in men	47–48

CHAPTER II. THE GUIDE BOOK.

The Book the key to life and the world	49–50
I. The Scriptures Revelation of God	51
1. The gods of the nations and the God of the Bible	52
2. God is in all things	53–54
3. Scripture gives us the key to life	55–58
4. It also interprets human experiences	59–61
5. The true use of Scripture	61–63
II. The Best Method of Studying Scripture	
1. By books for revelation	63
Prophet Hosea, Gospel of Luke	64–65
2. By characters for inspiration	67
Real men : Saint-making in process	68–69
Profitableness of biography	69
3. By topics for doctrine	70
This requires toil, but repays toil	72

ANALYSIS OF CONTENTS. iii

CHAPTER III. THE ROAD OVER CALVARY.

PAGE

The Cross a fact in experience and a law of life.
I. The Cross in Man's Redemption..........
  1. The cross reveals God.................. 75
    Creation God's self-revelation.......... 76
    Cross reveals holiness and love......... 78
  2. The cross delivers men from sin........ 79
    Shows nature of sin................... 80
    And delivers man from sin............. 82
  3. The cross brings God and man together 83
    Reconciliation and what it implies.... 84
II. The Cross the Disciple's Law of Life..... 85
  1. The being of God the law of the universe 85
    Christ honors law of cross............ 86
    And establishes as law for man........ 87
  2. Discipleship means acceptance of law
    of cross............................ 87-88
    Christian Christ continued............ 89
  3. Called to organize life on basis of sacri-
    ficial love........................... 90
    Law of Cain and law of Christ........ 91
    The power of the cross.. 92
    The cross life's glory and joy......... 93

CHAPTER IV. THE INNER ROOM.

The secret sources of character............... 94
I. The Three Reasons for Prayer...........
  1. The reason of human need............. 96
    Need creates obligation. 98
    Personal relations with God.......... 99
  2. In prayer God imparts his best gifts..... 100
    God's best gift himself................ 101
  3. In prayer blessings brought to others..... 101
Two objections to prayer :
  1. Objection in name of love.............. 102
  2. Objection in name of law.............. 103
    The true efficacy of prayer............ 105
II. The Three Elements of Prayer........... 106
  1. Worship 106
    Thankfulness and adoration.......... 107
  2. Confession......... 107
  3. Communion............................ 108-110

ANALYSIS OF CONTENTS.

	PAGE
III. The Three Kinds of Prayer	111
1. The prayer that is unheard	111
From disobedient, selfish heart; purely personal	112–115
2. The Gentile prayer	116
Temporal interests supreme	117, 118
3. The fully Christian prayer	118
Full of love for all men	119
Moves in realm of moral certainty	120

CHAPTER V. PAST THE DEAD POINTS.

Habit distributes men's power equally and regularly over life	123
I. The Law of Habit	124
Life builds itself up out of habits	124–126
Habit ensures permanency to life	127–129
II. The Place of Habit in Life	
1. In man's physical being	129
Illustrations: Hugo and Herodotus	130
2. In mental life	131
Genius and habit	132
3. In moral life	133
Conduct a fine art	134
III. The Right Habits to be Cultivated	135
1. Of prayer	136, 137
2. Of Bible study	138
3. Of Christian service	139
4. Of reading	140–142

CHAPTER VI. THE LESS HONORED VIRTUES.

The balance of virtues in Christian character	144
I. The place of the Passive Virtues	146
Different ideals of the world	146
The emphasis of Christianity	147–149
The efficiency of these virtues	150–153
Their place in Christian character	154–155
II. The Analysis of these Virtues	
Humility and pride	157, 158
Contentment and ambition	159–161
Patience and ill-temper	162–165
Character is Christian in so far as it is finer than other character	

ANALYSIS OF CONTENTS.

CHAPTER VII. THE TRANSFIGURED TASK.

	PAGE
The Christian sees all things in God............	167
I. The Christian Conception of Life........	
The Jewish idea......................	168
The Christian idea....................	169
The Apostle Paul's teaching...........	171, 172
Life not two hemispheres.............	174–177
II. The Application of the Christian Principle...............................	
Christianity an earth religion..........	178
Jesus doing the Father's will..........	179
The disciple's fidelity.................	180, 181
All life belongs to God...............	182
Each man's calling...................	183–186

CHAPTER VIII. THROUGH VANITY FAIR.

The Christian citizen and amusements........	188
I. The Christian citizen may enjoy life....	190
All extremes wrong...................	191
Christianity not a fast but a feast......	192, 193
Principles better than rules...........	195
1. Negatively.	
a. Avoid whatever endangers health	196
b. Shun questionable associations....	196
c. Avoid whatever arouses morbid appetite..............................	197
d. Shun what may cause others to stumble........................	197
2. Positively.	
a. Make recreation a means to an end.	198
b. Ministers to higher nature........	198
c. Makes life more joyous...........	199
d. Awakens soul.....................	200
II. The Christian Must Preserve his Integrity.	
Be true everywhere...................	201
Man and environment.................	202
The common excuse.....	204, 205
Whatever Christ expects is possible....	207

vi ANALYSIS OF CONTENTS.

CHAPTER IX. IN MILL AND MARKET.

	PAGE
Relation of trade and labor to moral character.	209
I. The Moral Significance of Trade and Labor..	209
Work is normal and necessary	210
Wrong conceptions of work	212
Christ ennobles all life	214
a. Meaning of work	215
b. Meaning of Trade	217
1. A man's calling his priestly service	218
2. Character is made and revealed in daily tasks	220
II. The Moral Principles for the Mill and Market	
The old and new economics	221
1. Every man should earn all he receives	224
Gambling and speculation	225
2. Every man should seek to render largest service	227
The Royal Law of Christ	228
3. No man should take advantage of another	229
Merchant of Alexandria	230
Love not selfishness basis of economics	231
Captains of Industry to organize society	233

CHAPTER X. THE CITIZEN AND HIS POLITICS.

The state one of three divine institutions	235
Life completed only in fellowship..	236
I. The Divine Meaning of the State	237
1. The organ of the political consciousness.	239
2. The institute of right relations	239
3. The partnership of men in all good	240, 241
An instrument of God's sovereignty.	242
The Biblical teaching	243
II. The Citizenship of the Christian Disciple.	245
Politics the science of social welfare	245
The obligations of popular government.	247, 248
1. The Christian a patriot	249
2. Governs himself by moral principles	250

ANALYSIS OF CONTENTS. vii

	PAGE
3. Endeavors to create better society	253
Knowledge of right call to service	255
Making the New City	258
The Kingship of Christ over the State	259

CHAPTER XI. THE PALACE BEAUTIFUL.

The Church a voluntary institution, but most necessary	261
I. The Church the Confession of the divine life in man	262
a. New life cannot be hid	262
b. Nature of spiritual life necessitates confession	263
c. Church organized witness for Christ	264
II. The Church the co-operation of men in behalf of holiness	267
a. Perfection comes through fellowship.	267
b. Through fellowship worship promoted.	268
c. The medium of mutual service and sacrifice	271
III. The Church the organized service of Christian discipleship	273
a. Church is Christ continued	274
b. Order and ordinances of the Church..	275
c. The three figures of Church's work	278
The Church essentially missionary and redemptive	280

CHAPTER XII. GAINING THE CROWN.

The future value of present resources	281
I. The Making of Character the Meaning of Life	
Three kinds of men	283 ✓
Character the supreme thing	285
Character is a creation	286
II. The World Designed for Making of Character	287 ✓
Is this the best possible world?	288
Life a school	289, 290
Conservation of energy	292–294
No mistake in human lot	295

ANALYSIS OF CONTENTS.

PAGE

III. The Well-made Character Fitted for High
Responsibilities..........................
Character a timeless thing.............. 298
Man's life made for two worlds......... 299
The universe in process of making..... 300
Traders now, rulers by and by.......... 300
Concluding word....................... 301

INTRODUCTORY.

WHENCE AND WHITHER.

I pray not that thou shouldst take them out of the world, but that thou shouldst keep them from the evil.—JESUS CHRIST.

Life consists in harmony with environment. The fullness of it is measured by the response that we make to the world about us. The clear sight of the eye, the keen hearing of the ear, the vigorous, intelligent, and delightful appreciation of the best in nature, in books, and in art, the right relation between a man and his neighbors, these things go to make up life.—GEORGE HODGES: *Faith and Social Service.*

To move among the people on the common street ; to meet them in the market-place ; to live among them not as a saint or monk, but as a brother man with brother men ; to serve God not with form or ritual, but in the free impulse of a soul ; to bear the burdens of society and relieve its needs ; to carry on the multitudinous activities of the city, social, commercial, political, philanthropic, in Christ's spirit and for his ends ; this is the religion of the Son of man, and the only meetness for heaven which has much reality in it.—HENRY DRUMMOND.

> Manhood's the one immortal thing
> Beneath Time's changeful sky.—ANON.

SPRINGTIME is old, yet ever new. The man who lives with open eye and receptive heart sees larger and deeper meanings in each returning springtime. The universe in which we live is the same universe that Adam saw and Solomon studied : but in the sciences of astronomy and geology it has become a greater and more wonderful universe.

"The eye," says an old proverb, "sees that which it brings with it the power of seeing." In himself Jesus Christ is the same yesterday, to-day, and forever. But in the nature of things, he grows upon men, as they grow in grace and truth and in the knowledge of his will. The Spirit takes of the things of Christ and shows them unto men, so fast and so far as they are able to bear them. Being a Christian in its inner significance is the same from century to century; but in its outward expression the Christian life means a very different thing from age to age. The new wine, the new glad life in Christ, which he imparts to all who believe in him, requires ever new and congenial modes of expression. So long as the new wine of the kingdom is being produced by the living and eternal vine of truth, so long will there be need of new bottles for its reception and preservation. The vine is old; the wine is new; and the bottles must be new.

Christianity, as Rothe suggests, is the least immutable thing in the world; and this is its peculiar glory. The words that our Master has spoken are spirit and they are life. The truth of Christ is spiritual and vital, it is personal and not propositional. By its very constitution Christianity is not something that can be settled once for all in some mould of thought, or some method of life. Geometry is a fixed science, but Christianity is not geometry. The truth of Christ is a seed and not a crystal; it is a principle of life and not a logical formula. It is a new light to every seeing eye, a new life in every renewed man, a new power in every age. We are thus prepared to expect varying interpretations of the Christian principle and diverse manifestations of the Christian life. The most striking feature of Christianity is its timeliness, its adaptedness to the changing conditions of life. The truth as it is in Jesus remains forever the same without increment or diminution. But men's apprehension and application of that truth vary with their changing conceptions and needs. Revelation, says the writer of the Epistle to the Hebrews, has come to men in divers portions and in divers fashions. As the revelation has been given, so has it become known; in many parts and in many ways. Each generation cherishes a few great texts and enters into their deeper meaning. The truth of Christ which that generation proves goes to make up the increasing sum of the things of Christ which are known to men. The truth of the kingdom is cast into the ground and springs up and grows, first the blade, then the ear, and after that the full corn in the ear. The Teacher expressly intimates that the truth of the kingdom is to be in every man and in every age as new wine, which ever requires new skins.

In nothing is the vitality and manifoldness of Christianity so manifest, as in the different ideals of character and sainthood which have held sway from age to age. As we survey these varying ideals, one might almost suppose that we were reviewing a series of different religions, rather than different expressions of the same religion. It may be worth our while, at the beginning of this study, to notice briefly the various ideals of the Christian life which have prevailed in the Christian centuries.

1. We go back to the church of the first three centuries, and we find ourselves in a very different atmosphere from the life of to-day. We find that the one supreme ideal of men in those centuries was a child-like humility and a submissive obedience. Men endeavored to keep themselves unspotted from the world, and in patience and humility they waited for their Lord's return. In those early centuries the Christians were known for their virtuous lives and loving fellowship. Fitness for church membership was proved by one's obedience to the plain moral requirements of the gospel. In singleness of heart, the disciples lived their lives in the sight of men ; with a deep love to the Lord Jesus and a firm hope of a life beyond the grave, they went about their duties or were led forth to martyrdom. Great emphasis all through these ages falls upon the moral conduct of the disciples. From the second century a remarkable document, "The Teaching of the Twelve Apostles," has come down to us. We may presume that this represents the manner of life and form of teaching in that age. This document begins by setting before us the two ways, one of life, and the other of death. The way of life consists in this :

"First, thou shalt love God who made thee; secondly, thy neighbor as thyself; whatsoever things thou wouldest not have done to thyself, do not thou to another." Then follows a general summary of the moral teachings of the sermon on the mount. In this age discipline was rigidly maintained in the church, and membership in the body of Christ was always based on the one matter of conduct. The church was a community of saints, and the aim of all was to practice the simple counsels of perfection. To be a member of this community of saints was to be a child of God, and an heir of unending life; to be excluded from this community was to be cast into the outer darkness with the dogs, and murderers, and idolaters. "They were baptized, not only into one body, but also by one Spirit, by the common belief in Jesus Christ as their Saviour, by the overpowering sense of brotherhood, by the common hope of immortality. Their individual members were the saints, that is, the holy ones. The collective unity which they formed—the church of God—was holy!" (Hatch: The Hibbert Lectures, p. 335). With more or less of variation this was the ideal of perfection and sainthood which dominated the thought and fired the heart of believers in the first three centuries.

2. But slowly another ideal comes to the front. Christianity has become diffused throughout the known world; but somehow the salt has not sweetened things; the leaven has not leavened society.

In the fourth century clouds begin to gather thick and dark over the fair and open sky. Within the Roman world, the stain of vice has gone so deep that there seems to be no hope of whitening society, and saving the world. The bonds of society are unloosed, and things are going to swift and hopeless decay. Far off on the horizon are now seen hordes of barbarians; with fierce faces and wild cries and cruel swords, they sweep down over the land to burn and pillage, to murder the men and carry off the women. The Church has itself become corrupted, and the clergy are too often profligate and faithless. "The Church was gradually transformed from being a community of saints— of men who were bound together by the bond of a holy life, separated from the mass of society, and in antagonism to it—to a community of men whose moral ideal and moral practice differed in but few respects from those of their Gentile neighbors. The Church of Christ, which floated upon the waves of this troublous world, was a Noah's ark, in which there were unclean as well as clean" (Hatch : The Hibbert Lectures, p. 339). Earnest men and women have come to feel that it is utterly vain and useless to make a stand against this universal corruption while remaining in it. The very heavens seemed about to fall upon this great sinning, cursing, intriguing, corrupting world. What could one do who wished to save his soul alive? How could one make his protest against the evils of his time? One thing, only one thing seemed possible and right: to flee from the world and from the city of destruction to the caves of the mountains and the homes in the desert, there to commune with God and to cultivate the graces of the Spirit. These men believe most firmly in a future life, and this other world now becomes the one object of their hope and longing. At any rate, by the close of the fourth century, the ascetic ideal was almost universally supreme. To be a saint one must unlock all earthly ties, come out from the world, and in some cave or cell, with much fasting and many prayers, prepare the soul for the other world to which it was hastening. The great duty of life is now preparation for quitting life. In one immortal poem, The Divine Comedy, Dante has summed up all the hopes, the ideals, the beliefs of ten centuries. Life to him has become a pilgrimage, and by weary rounds of toil and sacrifice he is led along the climbing way of holiness to the attainment of the Beatific Vision. Throughout all these centuries the men and women noted for their saintliness are the men and women who have adopted the ascetic life and lived in celibacy. "Instead of bringing the sanctions of the world beyond the grave to bear upon the establishment of universal justice and love, the other world was made the object of direct and exclusive longing. The present life was dwarfed; and it was taught that eternal happiness was to be gained, and misery avoided, by constantly dwelling upon eternity in a separate life of prayer and mortification" (Fremantle : The World as the Subject of Redemption, p. 168). The Christian's calling is preparation for quitting life.

3. The centuries pass ; and as they pass another ideal comes to the front. The church has now won a place for itself in the life of the world, and has become supreme over all human affairs. Every part of life is under the direction and authority of the church. At the Jubilee of 1300, Pope Boniface VIII. appeared crowned and sceptered, and laying his hand on a sword, said to the pilgrims : "I am Cæsar ; I am Emperor." The clergy make it the business of their lives to observe the elaborate ceremonials which have grown with the progress of the centuries. Great cathedrals are built where, in the dim and sacred light, men bow and adore the host. On the part of the people, there is the most unquestioned submission to all the rituals and ceremonials of the church. The one ideal dominating the minds of men is obedience to the clergy and full reverence for the church and her services. "The whole cycle of social and moral duty is deduced from the obligation of obedience to the visible autocratic head of the Christian state" (Bryce : The Holy Roman Empire, pp. 63, 64). These words apply to Charlemagne, but aptly describe the condition of things for many centuries. Church work, church ideas, church services have become something quite different from simple Christian goodness. In a word, it may be said that the great effort of great

clerical leaders "is to induce men not to consecrate their lives to God but to be obedient to the pope and the clergy" (Fremantle: Ibid. p. 189). The saint has become the submissive church devotee.

4. Then comes the Reformation, the great uprising of positive religious conviction. For a long time the individual has been nothing, lost in the life of the universal church. He had nothing to do but to submit himself to the clergy and to do as he was told. But in Martin Luther, in Balthasar Hubmaier, and in Calvin, the new ideas of the coming age find expression. See that solitary man at Worms facing the four hundred frowning dignitaries of the church: he holds in his arms a copy of the Scriptures, and gives a reason out of that book for the hope that is in him. Then with a reckless abandon he cries: "Here I stand; I cannot do otherwise; so help me God." Those words struck the key-note for the new age. After a long and painful experience, his soul has broken through the shows of things in which he has so long been ensnared, and he has come face to face with reality. He sees now that a man is justified by his own personal faith, and that each man has to do directly with the eternal God. The Reformation was in a large sense the discovery of the worth and place of the individual. The Scriptures are now placed in each man's hand, and he is bidden to read and believe for himself. Guizot has said that the great fact of the Reformation is con-

tained in one word—liberty. At any rate, with the Reformation there has come the discovery of the individual soul, and the assertion of the privilege of every man to be himself. Out of this passion for personality have come many reforms in church and state. Protestantism in religion is the obverse of Democracy in government. Men were consumed with a passion to make the most of themselves and for themselves; they became impatient of restraint, and insisted on the right of free thought and untrammeled action. For its time and place this was a great ideal, and it has played an important part in the drama of the world's development. Since the Reformation the Christian ideal has appeared as a great passion for personality, and a desire to be free from all traditions and restraints.

While these varying ideals have prevailed, now here, now there, let no one suppose that one has prevailed to the total exclusion of the others. As a rule they have been blended and interfused, more or less, in every man and in every age. But in their larger and more general characteristics, these are the ideals that have glowed before the minds of men. Each of these ideals has served a useful purpose; each has played an important part in the progressive life of the world; each has added something to the world's accumulating knowledge of the things of Christ. Now, however, the progress of the world and the inworking of the Spirit are slowly unveiling before men some great, new, glad ideal of the meaning of the Christian life, and the dignity of the Christian's calling.

5. And this brings us to consider that new ideal of Christian character, which the Spirit is making known to our generation. Upon the men of this generation a magnificent Christian truth is dawning in all the morning splendor of a glorious day. The race is painfully learning what has been called the sense of humanity. We are coming to see the full meaning of many of the great words of the Christian revelation given centuries ago, but only partially understood. We are coming to see a larger and higher meaning in those texts of Scripture which assert the unity of the race in sin and need and redemption. Very clearly the writers of the New Testament have set forth the truth that the centuries and the nations are bound together in the one bundle of life. They have taught us that humanity is a whole, of which the individual is a member, and that each is for all, and all for each. They taught that we are all unitedly to attain to the faith and knowledge of the Son of God, unto the measure of the stature of the fullness of Christ. They taught that the race is a unit, and that the first man's life is so linked in with the last man's life that one without the other cannot be perfect. In other words, no man can enter into the fullness of life and attain the beatific vision, till the whole people of God has reached its appointed goal.

To-day men are learning to think of humanity,

not as a series of disconnected individuals, but as the inter-related members of a living society. Each member supplements the other ; he lives himself by helping others live ; "all the body fitly framed and knit together through that which every joint supplieth, according to the working in due measure of each several part, maketh the increase of the body unto the building up of itself in love." (Eph. iv. 16. R. V.). Our personal life is rooted in the life of humanity; it flourishes in that soil, and draws its richest nourishment from it. The person comes to perfection only in and through fellowship. Man is a being of relationships. So long as those relationships are imperfect, we cannot have perfect men. God has so linked the race together by ties which cannot be broken, that no man can give the world the slip, cast off all human ties, and rise to fullness of perfection by himself. The time will never come, either here or hereafter, when the individual will attain to self-sufficiency, and grow to perfection through isolation. Love, beneficence, and righteousness will forever have meaning. Forever we shall be members one of another, and dependent the one upon the other. The perfection which Christ demands, and which creation awaits, is the perfection of humanity in the mutual supply of each member of that which is lacking in the others. The whole race is bound together in a community of interests and responsibilities. Thought is unable to conceive of any such thing as an independent being. A man out of relation with his fellows is not a man in all the meaning of that term. We begin life as sons; we continue it as brothers, fathers, neighbors. Father and mother are related to other families, and thus the circle widens out through the family, the community, the state, the race. The long lines of ancestry behind each one of us reach back into the past through countless generations, and form the woof on which the fabric of our humanity is woven.

"For mankind are one in spirit, and an instinct bears along,
Round the earth's electric circle, the swift flash of right or wrong:
Whether conscious or unconscious, yet humanity's vast frame,
Through its ocean-sundered fibres, feels the gush of joy or shame;
In the gain or loss of one race, all the rest have equal claim."
—JAMES RUSSELL LOWELL.

Upon the sight of men there now breaks the vision of humanity, by the services and sacrifices of each member, building itself up in love; a humanity in which each member, seeking the welfare of others, has supplied that which is lacking in himself; a humanity growing up into Christ in all things through the mutual exchange of spiritual services.

Once the Pilgrim's calling was conceived under the terms of escape from the city of Destruction. The awakened Pilgrim rushes out of the city putting his hands over his ears, crying, "Life, life, eternal life." That was a true ideal of life in certain times and places; it is true to certain experiences of the Christian life in every age. It has been pointed out as a grave defect in Bunyan's great allegory that Pilgrim never does anything but attend to the salvation of his own soul. His great thought by day, and his anxious dream by night, is escape from the city. When once entered upon the heavenward road he seems to forget his wife and children and friends. The criticism, as Professor Drummond shows, is hardly fair, as Bunyan was not attempting to give a complete picture of the Christian life; rather he was giving that life in one of its relations. The complete picture of the new Christian Pilgrim is that of a man who remains right in the midst of the city of destruction and plans and labors to transform it into the city of God. His progress in the divine life is to be measured by the way he fulfills his human relationships and infuses into his tasks the spirit of Christ. Instead of longing and praying to get away from earth to heaven, the New Pilgrim seeks to bring heaven down to earth, to build right here in these cities of earth the New Jerusalem with its peace and glory and love and righteousness. The vision of character is the vision of a man who accepts his human relationships and honors them; who endeavors to fulfill every relationship in the spirit of Christ and to attain unto a full-rounded human life.

And growth in grace and progress of character is to be measured by the degree in which one has fulfilled the relationships of his being Godward and manward. A man's relations to his fellowmen measure his relations with God his Father. "Hence our serviceableness to our fellow-men is the exact and infallible measure of our acceptableness to God" (Hyde : Outlines of Social Theology, p. 107). Before we can pronounce a man good at all, we must know how he is honoring the bonds in which he is related to his fellows. No man can stand right with God who does not seek to stand right with all mankind. The first great commandment is : "Thou shalt love the Lord thy God with all thy heart, and with all thy soul, and with all thy mind." And the second is like unto it, and equal to it : "Thou shalt love thy neighbor as thyself" (Matt. xxii. 37, 39). A man's love for his fellows is the test and measure of his love for God (1 John. iv. 7, 8). Religion is morality looking Godward ; and morality is spirituality looking manward. Apart from human life to act upon, apart from the relations of men with one another, there can be no such thing as Christianity. Men have sometimes thought of the Christian religion as something added on to life, something which can exist apart by itself, something which can be kept hidden in the soul : but this is totally to misapprehend its nature. Righteousness is the quality of rightness. Virtue is a matter of relations. Goodness is an attitude of soul. Character is the measure of one's social adjustments. And life, in the only definition which is satisfactory, is a matter of relationships. The degree of life is measured by the degree of correspondences with environment. It is not enough to know that a man is pure and reverent, prayerful and heavenly-minded; we want to know what kind of a man he is in the home, in the store, in the political primary; what kind of a father he is, what kind of a workingman, what kind of a voter, taxpayer, and citizen.

Jesus Christ came into the world to save men. But what do we mean by salvation? Not the mere transfer of the soul from one side to the other of a safety line, without touching any other life or affecting human relations. Salvation is a word with a tremendous scope and meaning. The mighty orbit of that word sweeps far beyond the individual life, it describes a circle whose circumference is as wide as the nature of man and as high as the thought of God. The one great aim of Christianity is to make men good; but what do we mean by goodness? What are the great virtues of the Christian life? Love, joy, peace, long-suffering, gentleness, goodness, fidelity, meekness, temperance, justice, generosity, forbearance, forgiveness, truthfulness,—these are the virtues which Scripture everywhere honors. And these virtues are matters of human relations and social adjustment. The man who is struggling to be right and to do right is struggling to stand foursquare with his fellows. The forms of evil that assail a man's virtue are social also; hatred, variance, emulations, wrath, strife, seditions, schisms, envyings, murders, drunkenness, revellings, and such like. Here, amid the throng and press of human interests and passions; here in this actual work-a-day world, amid the waves of public opinion and the eddyings of private affection; here, in these homes and stores and factories of earth, Christian character is to be formed and maintained. Its sphere of manifestation is human life with its interests and relations.

Before we can think rightly and justly of Christian character, we need to get rid of some of the traditions which have come down to us from the past. In the minds of many people, sainthood means a heavenly sweetness which nothing can ruffle, a serene brow, a peaceful heart, an unnatural calmness, an other-worldliness of temper and disposition. We are more impressed with a man's saintly character if he is somewhat pale and melancholy; and we do not expect him to have too much flesh on his bones. The saint of the middle ages, the saint that is to be seen pictured on the walls of cathedrals, the saint who yet haunts the imagination of men, has a thin pale face, with eyes red from weeping and watching, with wasted form and thin, transparent hands, who takes no interest in the everyday interests of common men, and dreams day and night of the city in the skies. One was reckoned a saint according to the degree of his isolation and insulation from the common affairs of ordinary men. Because of this mistaken conception, we have failed to canonize many of the best and greatest saints of God. A keen interest in the common work and common affairs of life was thought to be inconsistent with the life of faith and devotion. A modern writer has found fault with the character of Thomas Arnold for the simple reason that Arnold was "vigorous, youthful, eager, intense, lively, affectionate, hearty, and powerful." Dr. R. W. Dale quotes him as finding in this character a certain deficiency; there was not enough sadness in it to touch our deeper human sympathies. Canon Mozley, for it is he who finds fault with Arnold, says: "Arnold's character is too luscious, too joyous, too brimful. Head full, heart full, eyes beaming, affections met, sunshine in the breast, all nature embracing him—here is too much glow of earthly mellowness, too much actual liquid in the light" (Dale: Laws of Christ for Common Life, p. 227). Arnold would have come nearer his ideal of sainthood had he been less happy and human, more solemn, more otherworldly, more pale and sallow.

As Jesus Christ was in the world, so his disciples are called to be. The Master does not pray that his disciples be taken out of the world, but he does pray that they may be kept from the evil of the world. Jesus mingled with men in the most natural and human way, sharing their sorrows, participating in their joys, feeling their wrongs, grieved at their misdeeds, honoring all the relationships of life, and taking an interest in whatever concerned man. John the Baptist came neither eating nor drinking; he was an ascetic and a hermit. But Jesus came eating and drinking and making himself perfectly at home among men. Men dream of a sainthood to be won by insulating themselves from this great needy, groaning, cursing, dying world, and in isolation cultivating the graces of the Spirit, preparing themselves for another world; forever despising this world. More than one man has said to me that religion is a good thing for those who have time to cultivate it, but for hard-working men it does not answer very well. This is because men have a totally wrong idea of what religion is. Christianity is an earth religion, and has to do with the actual things and relations of everyday life, with such real things as homes and stores, factories, and counting rooms; with such real relations as buying and selling, marrying and giving in marriage, voting and working. Christianity is an effort to transmute and transfigure the dust of our humanity and the life of our world into the righteousness of the living God. By his life among men the Lord Jesus has touched with a divine beauty and filled with a divine splendor these common relations and occupations and interests of life. Christianity is the most real thing in the world. Christliness is the mould into which the whole creation is being shaped. Christian life is simply right life, life that has come to perfection. Christian character is the only right character, and it is Christian just so far as it is finer, stronger, better than other character.

But some one says, this is cheapening the gospel; this is making it such a real and commonplace thing; this is making Christian character an everyday matter. Precisely so; and this is just what Jesus Christ intends. "We treat God with irreverence," says Ruskin, "by banishing him from our thoughts, by not referring to his will on slight occasions. His is not a finite authority or intelligence which cannot be troubled with small things. There is nothing so small but that we may honor God by asking his guidance of it, or insult him by taking it into our own hands; and what is true of the Deity, is equally true of his revelation. We use it most reverently when most habitually; our insolence is in ever acting without reference to it, our true honoring of it is in its universal application" (Introductory to Seven Lamps of Architecture). The sainthood of the monk's cell is not half so fine a thing as the sainthood of the kitchen or the store or the political party, in which one may seemingly be less devout and other-worldly. It is comparatively easy to be devout, and sweet tempered and other-worldly in the monk's cell or the devotee's closet; but it is a finer, worthier, Christlier kind of sainthood to take an interest in whatever concerns man, to play a whole man's part in the world, and to war a good warfare with the evils of society. We call the missionary a hero and saint who gives up home and native land to preach the gospel to lost men in far off lands. He is a saint and a hero, and merits his crown. But who expects to find the hero and saint in the kitchen with hot, flushed face, fulfilling the duties of the home in the spirit of Christ? Who looks for the hero and saint in the merchant who is resolved to conduct his business as if Jesus Christ were his partner? Who discovers the saint and hero in the citizen who, in the face of misrepresentation and by many trials, is working for purer politics, better laws and cleaner literature? With many people spirituality means an isolation of one's self from the things of time, a cutting of the ties of earth, an other-worldliness of temper and thought. Spirituality is a tone of thought and not a zone of life.

Instead therefore of trying to disengage ourselves from the great web of human life, with its limitations, its heartaches, its burdens, its sins, let the man who would be true to the Master and win his crown, accept his place in the world, seek to honor all his relationships, and labor in all ways for the betterment of the world. The Christian disciple has no call to extricate himself from the world of which he is a part, disown all human ties, and live in isolation. He is called to remain right in the midst of the city of Destruction and plan and labor to transform it into the city of God. The character which we are to cultivate to-day is the character in the home, in the store, in the counting-room, the character of full-rounded human life. He has the finest Christian character who remains right in the world, who accepts his human lot and transfigures it; who bears the burdens and heartaches of society without losing heart; who fulfills every duty which life imposes in a faithful and loving spirit. One had better be content to forego a little tranquillity of soul and repose of life by remaining in the world, than to gain this tranquillity and repose by insulating one's self from his fellows. Very beautiful and striking is the story of the Buddhist saint who, by a long and weary round of fastings and prayers has reached the stage next to Nirvana. Now, by one decision, he can forever slip out of this troubled scene and be at rest. But he refused to make this decision, preferring to remain here where effort might bear fruit in other lives. "Not till the last soul in every earth and in every hell has found peace, can I enter on my rest." The place to meet Jesus Christ and to find his peace is in the path of service and common duty.

> The parish priest of Austerity
> Climbed up in a high church steeple
> To be nearer God, so that he might hand
> His word down to the people.
> And in sermon script he daily wrote
> What he thought was sent from heaven,
> And he dropped it down on the people's heads
> Two times one day in seven.
> In his age God said: 'Come down and die."

And he cried out from the steeple,
"Where art thou, Lord?" And the Lord replied,
"Down here among my people."

The subject of our study is the Forming and Maintaining of Character upon the Principles of the Bible. The thesis which we seek to develop is Learning the New Citizenship in the Kingdom of God is to Develop Right Christian Character. Such a character, being Christian, will find its ideals and sources in the principles of the Christian Scriptures. And such a character, being formed upon the principles of the Bible, will find its sphere of growth and manifestation in the daily round of life. Two things are especially emphasized.

1. Growth in character can best be promoted through the loving service of our fellows and the faithful fulfillment of the relationships of life. Many there are who go sadly and tragically wrong at this point. They are forever seeking to cultivate their spiritual life; they are agonizing to add a cubit to their spiritual stature; they long to perfect their spiritual character. "If any man willeth to do his will, he shall know of the teaching." Christian culture comes through Christian service. Perhaps the good Samaritan was thought by some of his pious friends to be a trifle lax in temple worship; it is certain that he could not repeat the Shibboleths of an exemplary Pharisee. It is quite possible indeed that he could not have done his temple devotions as zealously and exactly

as the Priest and the Levite with whom he is put in contrast on the Jericho road. Be that as it may, he was content to gain his spiritual culture through spiritual and loving service. One hour of such service as his on the Jericho road did more to add a cubit to his stature than a hundred years of temple droning, of spiritual self-analysis and self-vivisection. No man need fear that his spiritual culture will suffer by turning aside to help a fellow-creature. When Gregory the Great was told that a beggar had been found starved to death in the streets of Rome, he excommunicated himself for allowing such a thing to occur in a city under his care. He shut himself up in a cell, fasted and prayed, and sought to make atonement for his sin of omission toward the poor starveling.

2. Christian character is to be formed right in the stress and struggle of this world : it is to be maintained in the mill and in the store ; it is to be measured by the degree in which one fulfills his human relationships. Christian character is not something added on to life, not some special accomplishment like music or poetry. It is the harmonious development of the soul in all its powers and faculties ; it is the soul honoring and fulfilling all the relationships of life. The man lives in the world, but he lives a life whose springs are far away in the mountains of God ; he frames a character which is built after the pattern shown in the mount. Christian character is simply life come to its maturity and fulfillment.

THE NEW CITIZENSHIP.

CHAPTER I.

VISIONS AND IDEALS.

And look that thou make them after the pattern which was showed thee in the mount.—JEHOVAH TO MOSES.

Thin of Buddha, and you become like Buddha; if you pray to Buddha and do not become like Buddha, the mouth prays and not the heart.—*Buddhist Precept.*

In the outer limits of the intelligible world is the idea of good; an idea which is perceived with difficulty, but which when perceived, compels the conclusion that it is the ultimate cause of everything beautiful and good that is to be found in the universe: that in the visible world it produces light, and the star from which this directly comes; that in the invisible world it gives rise to truth and intelligence; finally, that we must have our eyes steadfastly fixed upon this idea if we wish to conduct ourselves wisely in public or private life.—PLATO: *Republic.*

> Ah, but a man's reach should exceed his grasp,
> Or what is heaven for?—ROBERT BROWNING.

RIGHT thought goes before right action. "Our wishes," some one has said, "are the forefeelings of our capabilities." All fine and effective work begins in an idea. The picture is older than the paint and canvas. The plans and specifications are antecedent to the building. As the seed cast into the ground dreams of the sunlight and the wheat field; so the germ of the ideal in the heart of man dreams of the future where it will have full scope. No man is better than his best thoughts. No life rises higher than its ideal. The boat that drifts, always drifts down stream. We do not want to drift; we do want to be true disciples; then we must have a care for the ideals and visions we cherish. A great many lives make sad shipwreck of themselves, and waste all their powers and talents, all because they lack a high ideal. Has a man an ideal in life? Has he a vision of something better and nobler? The answer to these questions will tell the whole story of his worth or worthlessness; it will determine his progress or his decline in the right life.

I. THE NECESSITY OF RIGHT IDEALS.

The man who can dream well is sure to get on in the world. He has a reason for living, and a power for progress. Because of his visions it is worth while for him to try to live a man's life. John Ruskin, in one of his suggestive lectures on art, has very clearly shown the reason why some nations have made no progress in art, while others have carried art to its highest perfection. He sums up his conclusions in words like these: Whenever art is practised for art's sake, and for the delight of the workman in what he does and produces, instead of in what he interprets and reveals, there art has a most fatal influence on heart and brain, and becomes the destruction both of intellectual and moral power. On the other hand, art that is devoted humbly and self-forgetfully to a statement and interpretation of the facts of the universe is always helpful and beneficent to mankind, and is sure to advance towards perfection. To illustrate this truth, he shows two old pieces of work taken from the early stages in art in their respective nations. These two pictures show clearly the difference between conventional art and progressive art. The first piece, made in Ireland, is taken from a Psalter of the eighth century, and is intended to represent an angel. This belongs to what Ruskin calls an utterly dead school of art. A figure is drawn very much in the shape of a pyramid, with an almost circular affair crowning it, representing the head. The lines of one side of the figure are exactly matched by the lines of the other side. The fingers taper to a point, and in each palm are three red spots. The eyes are simple circles with a circular dot in the centre, the head is surmounted with a curious covering, and there is no mouth to this strange being. Every line of the figure is formal, mathematical, lifeless. It is evident that the artist has simply tried to draw a few lines and circles, and that he had no great idea that he wanted to represent. From such beginnings, says Ruskin, no good art can ever come.

The other picture belongs to a very different order of work, and is taken from the church of St. Ambrogio at Milan. The artist has tried to portray the serpent beguiling Eve. The work is exceedingly crude, and the lines are rough and imperfect. But there is not a conventional or dead line in it. It is clear that the artist is laboring to express an idea that is far above his power of execution. He is not thinking of his lines but of his idea. To the people who thus begin, says Ruskin, nothing can be impossible; everything is prophetic and contains the promise and potency of a better day. The conclusion is clear: the man or the people satisfied with themselves and with their work never advance; it is only those who have an ideal which is far beyond them, who really struggle on and struggle up into life and perfection.

A man's ideal is his reason for living. We are justified by faith, says the Apostle. But what is faith, this faith that justifies? Faith is a vision of the soul, an aspiration after moral goodness. "Faith," says George Matheson, "is the sight of the moral ideal. To believe in Christ is a sign of moral goodness because it is a belief in moral purity." The man who has this sight of the moral perfection of Jesus Christ, and makes choice of him,—that man is justified by faith. Heaven estimates our worth or worthlessness not by what we are, but by what we are going to be. The man who really believes in Christ, "believes in the beauty of goodness, in the desirableness of purity, in the right of righteousness to be ultimately triumphant" (Matheson Landmarks of New

Testament Morality, p. 108). We are justified, not because we have any merit of our own, but because we see the merit of Jesus Christ, and make choice of him. You look at a little shoot just breaking through the ground, and you say it is an oak. Between that shoot and the great spreading tree there is a vast distance of years and growth; but in that shoot there is all the promise and prophecy of the full-grown tree. Here in the heart of man is hidden a little germ of faith in the Son of man. But the great Father, as he bends down in love over his child, sees in that germ the pledge of likeness to himself. To see Jesus Christ in this moral way is already to be in possession of his spirit. So the man is justified by his vision of Christ's love and purity and goodness, and his choice of that vision.

See those two men praying in the temple. There stands the Pharisee praying with himself, flattering himself, comparing himself with the men around, and thoroughly satisfied with himself. He stands the comparison pretty well; there is no doubt about that. But he is so good, so well satisfied with himself, that he will never be any better. Off in a corner stands a poor publican in a very different frame of mind. He forgets all about the attainments and failures of other men, and thinks only of God and of God's requirements. As men estimate things, his life will not compare very favorably with that of the Pharisee. But his one great aspiration is to keep step with the infinite God. What wonder that, out of a great, deep sense of shortcoming, he should cry: "God be merciful to me a sinner"? "I tell you," said Jesus Christ, and he knew, "this man went down to his house justified rather than the other." Better, like the Publican to aspire after God, and smite the breast with a painful sense of shortcoming, than to be satisfied with being as good as other men, and never become any better. Better, infinitely better, to be forever tormented by "the malady of the ideal," than to compare one's self with other lives, and feel the need of nothing. Better, immeasurably better, to live on the small arc of an infinite circle, than to compass the whole area of a three-foot circumference. Better be the least in the kingdom of heaven with an outlook as wide as eternity, than to be a king among men, with a horizon bounded by the cradle and the grave. Lowell is right,

"Not failure but low aim is crime."

The least in the kingdom of God is greater than the greatest outside that kingdom. Why? Because he has a wider outlook, a higher aspiration, a larger opportunity.

No man is ever better than his best thoughts. Professor Hart has said: "Great ideas precede and cause great achievements. The ideal Achilles made the real heroes of Marathon and the Granicus" (Life of Shakespeare). Let no Christian disciple be afraid to dream and to cherish his ideals. " Where there is no vision the people perish." The ideals of a nation are more important than its laws and legislatures. Youth especially is the time of aspiration and idealism. But the prophet Joel foresaw a day when young men shall see visions, and old men shall dream dreams. Let every one then, of whatever age, who would advance, who would be that great and wonderful thing God meant him to be, not fear to cherish his finest and highest ideals. These ideals and visions are the breath of eternity blowing across the stagnant marshes of this world to cleanse and purify them. Let a man give his ideals a chance to develop in all their glory and luxuriance. It will be time enough to hesitate and trim and creep when life is half over. Never mind if men do call him a dreamer of dreams. Once upon a time ten men mocked a younger brother because he dreamed great dreams. They envied him at first, and then went on to hate him. But the dreamer dreamed on, and the time came when they were willing to bow at his feet and acknowledge him as brother.

Everything worth doing in this world has been done by a "dreamer." America was a dream to Columbus long before it was a land to Europe. The thoughts of youth, Longfellow says, are long thoughts. The world is yet in its springtime, and everything worth doing and thinking has not been done. Life is full of unexhausted possibilities. Do not believe the words of the man who would tell you that the future of this world is mainly in the past, who says that there is nothing more to be known of God, nothing more to be seen in Christ, nothing heroic to be done for the kingdom. The man of visions will find that he has a hard time of it in this hard, matter-of-fact, prosaic world. Men will pity him, and will say, half in compassion, half in despair: "Oh, yes, I once, like you, had my dreams and visions, but life has knocked them all out of me. Cherish your dreams while you can, but let me tell you, they are but dreams and delusions." Too often youth is chilled and discouraged by these dismal words, and begins to pitch the life at a lower note. Slowly the ideals and aspirations of the heart begin to droop and die like flowers before an arctic wind. It is not easy to keep the vision and hopefulness of youth right on to the end of life; but the Christian must dare to do it. A Christian is a supreme idealist; he is one who lives for an ideal. Someone has spoken of Jesus of Nazareth as "That Good Idealist." We need not fear the term.

> "It takes a soul
> To move a body: it takes a high-souled man
> To move the masses even to a cleaner sty;
> It takes the ideal to blow an inch inside
> The dust of the actual."

The man who enters into God's plan and purpose, and cherishes his visions and ideals, can keep a sunny face and a cheerful heart all the way to the glory land.

II. The Ideals that are to be Cherished.

First of all, one must cherish a high ideal of the worth and meaning of life itself. In all ages there have been men who have affected to despise life, and have spoken slightingly of it. The book of Ecclesiastes is full of this despair of life. Everything is old, the sun is old, life is old, love is old, everything is in its last stage, every mine has been worked out, every song has been sung, nothing remains for man but warmed-over dishes. "Vanity of vanities, all is vanity." Man is nothing, as one end comes alike to man and dog. The dead are better off than the living, for they have done with this wearisome thing called life. The preacher is weary of everything, weary of knowledge, weary of fame, weary of effort, weary of wine and women, weary of watching the ways of men, weary of observing the beauty of the world, weary of earth's palaces and gardens. "All is vanity and vexation of spirit." This book, says Dr. R. W. Dale, was written, not by a great saint, but by a great sinner.

This conception of life has found many expressions in all ages and lands. Hear Kirke White cry :

> "What is this passing life?
> A peevish April day;
> A little sun, a little rain,
> And then night sweeps along the plain,
> And all things fade away."

Hear Byron, out of his disgust of life, say :

> "Count o'er the joys thine hours have seen,
> Count o'er thy days from sorrow free,
> And know, whatever thou hast been,
> 'Tis something better not to be."

Hear also Shakespeare make Macbeth lament:

> "To-morrow, and to-morrow, and to-morrow,
> Creeps in this petty pace from day to day
> To the last syllable of recorded time;
> And all our yesterdays have lighted fools
> The way to dusty death. Out, out brief candle!
> Life's but a walking shadow, a poor player,
> That struts and frets his hour upon the stage,
> And then is heard no more; it is a tale
> Told by an idiot, full of sound and fury,
> Signifying nothing."

Now, the Christian disciple must refuse to believe one word of this. Life is not a vanity and a cheat, and the things that men do and dream are not delusions. Life is infinitely worth while to the man who will make it so. Life is not a cheap and empty thing, but a divine thing full of divine surprises. Far truer, far more Christian than these dismal and godless views of life is the word of Browning, that man who believed in love and was very sure of God.

> "Grow old along with me.
> The best is yet to be,
> The last of life, for which the first was made;
> Our times are in his hand
> Who saith: "A whole I planned,
> Youth shows but half, trust God, see all, nor be afraid."

Again, he says in a final confession of his faith:

One who never turned his back but marched breast forward,
Never doubted clouds would break,
Never dreamed, though right were worsted, wrong would triumph,
Held we fall to rise, are baffled to fight better,
    Sleep to wake.

" No, at noonday in the bustle of man's work time,
Greet the unseen with a cheer!
Bid him forward, breast and back as either should be,
'Strive and thrive.' Cry, 'Speed,—fight on, fare ever,
    There as here.' "

Again, one needs to cherish an ideal of truth and duty. Truth is the most precious thing in the world, and in all ages has been the one object of search by philosophers and prophets, poets and thinkers. That old, old question of Pilate's—half sneering, half hopeless—has been repeated again and again: What is truth? Before one has lived long in the world he will find men who are skeptical concerning the reality of truth. They have mingled much with the world of men and things; they have gone behind the scenes and have watched the players making up for their parts; they have mixed with the world's business and politics, and know how false are many current opinions; they are acquainted with the books and papers of the day, and know how crude and hasty are the ideas put forth with so much flourish; they have used their reason and have found many of the common opinions of men utterly incapable of proof. And now at last they find themselves where Pilate stood, sure of nothing, questioning everything. One of these thinkers has told us that every candid thinker will admit that a universe may exist where two and two do not make four, and where two straight lines may enclose a space. Surely the man who could believe that ought to have no difficulty with the gospel story, miracles and all; nay, he ought to be able to accept the Apocryphal books in the bargain. The meanest demon in the brood is Mephistopheles, the mocking spirit that denies, for the sake of denying.

Before one has gone far through life he will find many lights arise and shine before him, each claiming to be the pole star. I remember a picture which I saw when a boy, of a man crossing a swamp at night, who sees before him a bright light, apparently of a lantern sent to show him the way across the bog. But, alas, it was but an *ignis fatuus*, a will-o'-the-wisp born of the swamp itself. Some of the fires the boys kindle on election nights seem brighter and larger than the eternal stars in God's heaven. And very often men are dazzled by these bonfires, and lose sight of the pole star. But soon the brave fire dies down to ashes, and lo, high above burns the star to guide lost and weary travelers safe home. The smoke of our bonfires may hide for a time the heavens, but be sure that above the smoke the stars are shining on in their calm depths, unchanged and unchangeable. To be brave and true one must cherish the ideal of truth, even in the darkest and gloomiest night. Believe in truth : believe that it is the only thing in the world worth possessing : believe that the search for it is the finest work of mortal man. Cherish the confidence that there are some things in this world worth living for and worth dying for. Be willing to have done with half truths and delusions, and be willing to follow truth to the ends of the earth. Know that nothing in this universe is so mighty as truth ; know also that a lie is weak though it have all the fleets and armies of the world behind it. The eternal years of God are truth's.

And last of all, cherish the ideal of progress. The worst form of unbelief is unbelief in the future and the better. There are men who tell us that all things are going wrong in this world, who assert that things are going to swift and hopeless decay. "O my soul, come not thou into their counsel ; unto their assembly, mine honor, be not thou united." The man who despairs of the future is lost to all high endeavor and hopeful living. The Christian disciple must not listen to the whispers of mutiny in the ranks, but must heed the inspiring call of the leader, as he summons him forward in the name of the Lord. There are many things in the world that cause serious misgiving and fear. Look at the lives blighted and blasted in our brightest civilization ; think of the dram-shop where manhood and hope and eternity are thrown away; go through one of our great cities and see thousands of lives out of whom poverty and misery have crushed all hope and self-respect; consider how the great Christian nations of the world are increasing their armies and navies, and are multiplying the means of destruction. In the face of these things, it is not easy to believe in progress and perfection. Many a light-hearted person has started out in life ignorant of the world, full of hope and enthusiasm, expecting that at his approach the evils and miseries of the world will strike tent and vanish. Soon or late one sees things as they are. Now with the facts of life full in sight dare one hope? Dare he cherish his ideal of progress? This is the trial of faith; this is the trial of every new age.

> "I slept and dreamed that life was beauty;
> I woke and found that life was duty."

On all sides we are told that the world is old, that we have come to the end of the ages, that our civilization has exhausted itself, and now nothing is before us but degeneration and darkness. But one must steadfastly refuse to give place to these gloomy and despairing views of life. He must cherish a passionate faith in progress; he must believe that a better order is coming to the birth out of the travail and pain of our age. Suppose that a treatise written by some intelligent spectator of the Paleozoic age had come down to us. In it he describes the mighty convulsions of that period, when continents are sunk here and upheaved there, when great volleys of lightning threaten to tear the very heavens asunder, when volcanoes below answer the fire above, when chaos seems about to come again at any moment. No doubt in such a treatise we should have many ominous laments over the changes and convulsions that threaten to overwhelm all life in a universal holocaust of death. Yet, to us looking back through the ages of geologic history and change, we see that out of the convulsions of that age there came the Mesozoic age, one step higher in the world drama.

> " Eternal process moving on,
> From state to state the spirit walks;
> And these are but the shatter'd stalks,
> Or ruin'd chrysalis of one."
> —TENNYSON: *In Memoriam*, lxxxii.

Whatever is wrong cannot be eternal; and whatever is right cannot be impossible. To believe this is faith; to live for this is Christianity.

III. THE TRANSFORMING POWER OF A RIGHT IDEAL.

A man's life is the incarnation of his thoughts, and ideals. What was only a dream yesterday becomes a resolve to-day, and an act to-morrow. We become like that which we habitually admire and desire. Hawthorne's beautiful allegory of the Great Stone Face expresses one of the profoundest truths of life. A suggestive writer tells this story of two women who lived in the same house; they were cousins. One slept in a room where she could look upon a picture of Marie Antoinette; the other had placed a picture of Joan of Arc at the foot of her bed. Each girl, on opening her eyes in the morning, looked upon a picture; one saw Marie Antoinette, and the other Joan of Arc. The one became deeply interested in the character of the beautiful queen, and read everything she could find concerning her, the times, the court in which she moved; she became familiar with all the vice and viciousness of the court of Louis XVI. The other became as deeply interested in Joan of Arc, and read everything she could find that gave her information concerning this pure, heroic, unselfish woman. The one who looked upon the picture of Joan of Arc became one of America's most devoted and useful women, one whose name carries benediction wherever it is mentioned. The other became one of the worst of characters, whose life was full of shame and sin. Constant and continued looking upon these two pictures, and dwelling upon the lives back of them greatly influenced two lives, leading one up into the highest womanhood and the other down into the deepest shame. (Possibilities, McClure, p. 70.)

There is no mystery about this. All literature, all life, illustrates this truth. Lowell's poem, "Longing," is only one writing among many others that might be named.

> "Still, through our paltry stir and strife,
>   Glows down the wished Ideal,
> And Longing moulds in clay, what life
>   Carves in the marble real.
> To let the new life in, we know
>   Desire must ope the portal;
> Perhaps the longing to be so,
>   Helps make the soul immortal."

The moment we think about it, we can easily see why Jehovah forbade the Israelites to make or to worship any graven image, or the likeness of anything that is in heaven above, or in the earth beneath, or in the water under the earth. The image at once limited the idea of God and reacted upon the life and imagination of the worshiper. No man ever became better than his best thought of God. There is a breadth, a freedom, a spontaneity, a progress in the life of the Jewish nation, that is utterly lacking elsewhere. No doubt much of this is owing to the ideal of God which dominated the thought and life of that wonderful people. Men grow into the likeness of that which they admire. An old whaling captain, when urged to give his heart to the Lord said: "Heart? I have no heart; if you should open my breast you would find nothing there but the image of a whale." In one of the galleries of Europe there hangs a striking picture. St. Anthony of Padua is preaching from the text: "Where your treasure is, there will your heart be also." Another compartment of the picture represents a man laid out for burial, surrounded by friends who are puzzled to know what was the cause of his death. A postmortem examination has been held, and the physicians are surprised to find that the man's heart has entirely disappeared. In another part of the picture we see the friends, acting upon the suggestion of the preacher, opening the dead man's money box, and finding the missing heart upon the pile of gold. No man ever rises above the heights of his habitual thought. "Show me a contented slave," said Burke, "and I will show you a degraded man." The best definition that I have ever seen of slavery was that given by an old ex-slave: "It took away all the to-morrows."

Being a Christian disciple and becoming like one's Lord is simply beholding the ideal of life as it is presented to us in the supreme life. "We all with unveiled face, reflecting as a mirror the glory of the Lord, are transformed into the same image, from glory to glory, even as from the Lord the Spirit" (R. V.). This process is deeper, more vital, more inward than imitation of the character of Jesus Christ. Imitation is mechanical and formal; this transformation is vital and organic. Imitation of Christ, adopting a figure, is the child attempting to reproduce the outlines of the landscape with pencil and paper. Assimilation of the character of Christ is the landscape imprinting itself by the unerring pencil of light upon the sensitized photographic plate. Imitation is the man trying to change himself; transformation is the man being changed by the power of the Spirit. In the one case the man goes to Christ and endeavors to copy the likeness he sees: in the other case the man allows Christ to come to him and to impress himself upon the soul. We are changed by beholding. The recognition of this fact would save the soul much anxiety, much fruitless effort. The Christian life is not living at random. No, it is contemplation of the glory of the character of Christ till one is transformed into the same image from glory unto glory. To become like Christ is the end of man; it is the only thing in life that is worth while; beside this all other efforts and achievements are petty and vain. Professor Drummond tells of a famous statue in the Galerie des Beaux-Arts in Paris, the last work of a great genius who, being very poor, lived in a garret in one room that served as studio and sleeping room. When the statue was finished, one night there fell a sudden and heavy frost upon the land. The sculptor lay awake in his cold room and thought of the moist clay, how the water would freeze in the pores and destroy in an hour the dream of a lifetime. So he arose from his bed and heaped the bed-clothes reverently and carefully round his work. In the morning, when the neighbors entered the room, they found the artist dead; but his statue lived. "Till Christ be formed in men, no man's work is finished, no religion is crowned, no life has fulfilled its end." For the attainment of this end every other plan and project must stand aside and take a subordinate place. For the achievement of this result every veil must be taken away from before the eyes and the soul must gaze with unveiled face upon him. As the plant in the window grows toward the light : so the soul grows toward him whom it loves and desires. Forty days Moses communed with God on the mount, contemplating the glory of the Lord. When he came down from the mount his face shone, so that the children of Israel could not look upon it. "His servants shall serve him and they shall see his face ; and *His name shall be in their foreheads.*"

CHAPTER II.

THE GUIDE BOOK.

>Thy word is a lamp unto my feet,
>And a light unto my path.—*The Psalmist.*

The knowledge of God without that of our misery produces pride. The knowledge of our misery without that of God gives despair. The knowledge of Jesus Christ is intermediate, because therein we find God and our misery.—BLAISE PASCAL.

Ay, that old Book, *That* shall be the source of our safety and of our greatness. Amid all the conflicts of the nations that are coming upon the earth, that Book shall be our life, our light, our security, our joy, our pillar of cloud by day, our pillar of fire by night, our guide through all our perils; and it will be found in that great day that none but those who are engaged in this work, none but those who have the Bible in their hands and in their hearts, will be able to meet the great conflict, and stand in their lot at the end of the days.—THE EARL OF SHAFTESBURY

All that I have taught of art, everything that I have written, every greatness that has been in any thought of mine, whatever I have been in my life, has simply been due to the fact that when I was a child my mother daily read with me a part of the Bible, and daily made me learn a part of it by heart.—JOHN RUSKIN.

THROUGHOUT the land of Egypt, that land of antiquity and mystery, there are the ruins of many temples and monuments. In many cases the walls of these are covered with pictures and hieroglyphics, which had for generations been objects of interest to travelers, but hopeless puzzles to scholars. Efforts had been made, and made almost in vain, to find the key to these mysterious writings. But, in 1799, a French engineer found at Rosetta a large black stone, much mutilated, but covered with figures and writings. This stone was taken to the British Museum and at once became an object of engrossing interest. It was seen to contain a trilingual inscription, in hieroglyphics, demotic, and Greek. By a careful study and comparison of these inscriptions, the key to the old Egyptian hieroglyphics was discovered, and the key to the writings on the monuments was in men's hands. With this alphabet, by means of this key, the mysterious writings have been read and the secrets so long hidden have become plain. By means of that little Rosetta stone, the life, the thought, the history of the men of a far-off age have been opened to the light of men of this generation.

What the Rosetta stone is to the old Egyptian hieroglyphics, the Christian Scriptures are to human life. As the Rosetta stone has given men the key to the old Egyptian language; so the Scriptures have given them the key to human life and destiny. In the Bible we have the record of God's dealings with one nation and a few individuals; but all these things, we are told, are types and ensamples unto us. A type is an example, a specimen, a pattern of something beyond itself. The Bible is the most human, the most divine book in the world. The things that are recorded in its pages are types and examples of what God is ever doing in man and for man. It is a revelation of God, of man, and man's experience of God. To understand the world of men and things, we must look at them from the divine side as well as from the human. Such a point of observation we have in the Scriptures. This gives the Scriptures such a supreme interest and supreme value; this makes them the key to man's experiences and the guide of man's life. It may not be amiss to consider the great purpose of the Scriptures; and the best way to use them for our largest profit.

I. THE SCRIPTURES ARE A REVELATION OF GOD.

One day, an intimate friend of the poet Tennyson said to him: "My dearest object in life, when at my best, is to leave the world, by however little, better than I found it; what is yours?" And Tennyson made answer: "My greatest wish is to have a clearer vision of God." We feel at once that the great poet had chosen the larger and better part. The greater includes the less. That man who has a clear vision of God will meet all the tests of a right life. The knowledge of God is the one deepest and most constant need of the world.

1. Men in all ages and in all lands have believed in a God; they have discerned his eternal power and Godhead in the things of creation. But this knowledge of God is not sufficient. To know that there is a God above us who has all power, brings little comfort and gives no hope. We want to

know what is the moral character of this God ; we want to know what is his disposition toward man ; we want to know what we may hope and what we should fear. The gods of antiquity, one and all, it has been clearly shown, were either non-moral or immoral. Jehovah is the only one who is conceived of as essentially and eternally moral. No man in the old world ever expected his god to be good and true ; a religious man in the ancient world did not need to be a good man. The gods of India, of Greece, of Rome, of Phœnicia, of Assyria and Babylon, one and all were immoral, lustful, dishonest, deceitful, indifferent to man and supremely selfish. The gods of antiquity lived

> " Careless of mankind,
> For they lie beside their nectar, and the bolts are hurled
> Far below them in the valleys, and the clouds are lightly curled
> Round their golden houses, girdled with the gleaming world ;
> Where they smile in secret, looking over wasted lands,
> Blight and famine, plague and earthquake, roaring deeps and fiery sands.
> Clanging fights, and flaming towns, and sinking ships, and playing hands—
> But they smile."

Here and there some god or goddess was interested in some man or tribe ; but love and holiness, as elemental facts of godhead, it never entered into the minds of men to conceive. Prometheus, one of the lesser gods, sees man destitute, cold, shivering, and with uncooked food. In pity he steals fire from heaven and gives it to man. For this deed of pity he is condemned by Jupiter, the father of gods and men, to be chained to Mount Caucasus to be torn of vultures. But over against all these conceptions of God, we place the Christian revelation. We find that this revelation is freighted with two great truths about God : he is holy, and he is love. These two truths really compose the Christian revelation of God. Revelation is not given primarily that we may know the power and eternity of God ; the Bible nowhere specially emphasizes these things ; these things, Paul says, can be known from the things which are made. But two great ideas dominate the Scriptures from beginning to end : his holiness and his love. In every religion the idea of God is the determinative element. In its conception of Godhead, Christianity differs a whole diameter from all other religions. Outside of the Christian revelation there is no conception of God which is worthy either of God or of man.

2. And this God is eternally active in the world, and continuously present in all things. One great purpose of Scripture is to show us how continuously active God is in his world. He is the life of the universe, the cause of its continuance from moment to moment. We live in what is called a scientific age, an age in which men are busy reading nature's secrets and formulating her laws.

We speak much of the laws of nature and talk learnedly of cause and effect. But we must never lose sight of the fact that God is ever active in all things, and what we call laws of nature are but the expression of his will and the signs of his presence. The Bible goes right to the root of the matter and says, God. God thundered; God sent the rain; he sends the sunlight streaming over hill and valley; he feeds the ravens and makes the lilies grow. Not a sparrow falleth to the ground without him. Changeless law is the unchanging purpose of the everlasting Father. The world is crowded full of God. In all things, through all things, in the swing of the heavenly body in its orbit, in the swelling of the tiny seed cast into the ground, in the opening rosebud, in the gathering dew and the falling rain, in the morning sunbeam and the evening flush upon the sky, there shines out the glory and perfection, and there is manifest the presence and activity of an infinite majesty. From moment to moment he is revealed in every mighty throb of rhythmic life throughout the universe. "The heavens declare the glory of God, and the firmament showeth his handiwork." "The fulness of the whole earth is his glory." The whole world is full of God, throbbing with his life and revealing his presence. The music of the running brook sings of him who is the soul of music. The glory of the sunset sky tells of him whose person is all glorious. The procession of the stars and the outgoings of the morning remind us of him who is the All-orderly, and whose works are all in truth.

"God is law, say the wise; oh, soul, and let us rejoice—
For if he thunder by law the thunder is yet his voice."

This truth is not poetry and word painting; no, it is the most literal fact, the blessed truth made plain in the Christian revelation.

3. Again; the Scriptures give us the key to the interpretation of human life. In the Scriptures a few men pass before us, and by means of the events recorded and the lives reflected there, we are enabled to interpret our own lives. By the aid of this book we learn how to estimate men's lives and characters; we are given the standards of the great white throne and the issues of the judgment day.

A few illustrations will make plain this truth. In the eyes of men, John the Baptist was neither great nor successful. To be sure, he had a momentary success; crowds gathered around him at the Jordan and hundreds accepted baptism at his hands. But in a few months his popularity is over; his most intimate followers have left him to follow another. Finally, in Herod's prison his life goes out in failure and defeat. A few disciples came and took up his body for burial; that was all. No nation mourned him; no monument was erected to his memory. Yet One who looked at men from heaven's side has pronounced his eulogy: "Verily, I say unto you, among them that are born of women there hath not risen a greater than John the Baptist." One day two men went up to the temple to pray. In a conspicuous place stands the Pharisee, and off in some corner stands the publican. Each is doing his devotions; each is reaching out after God. All goes on in silence; no man hears the prayers that go up from the two men. But the Master sees and hears; and he gives us a look at these men as they appear from heaven's side; we hear the prayers as they are heard in heaven. And somehow the men seem to be changing places, and we find ourselves saying with the Master: "I tell you this man went down to his house justified rather than the other."

Another time the Master tells of two men whose earthly conditions were very unlike. One man was a beggar, who lay at the rich man's gate, full of sores, desiring merely to be fed with the crumbs falling from the rich man's table. His condition is utterly sad and wretched, and not a man in the world would be willing to change places with him. One night he crawled under a hedge and died, with no one to fan his fevered brow, with no one to catch his farewell words. But one little line is given out of his biography as it is written in heaven: "He was carried by the angels into Abraham's bosom." Within the palace lives a rich man, happy and contented, with silks adorning his person, and with plenty of friends to sit at his table and honor his success. By and by sickness came to the palace; then with hushed voices and silent footsteps men came and went, and all the neighbors inquired how the sick man was doing. But it came to pass the rich man also died, and was buried. There were the forty days of mourning for him, the long procession to the grave and the costly monument. A leading citizen, a rich neighbor, a prominent business man has died. But we read on : "And in hell he lifted up his eyes, being in torment."

Up in Galilee lived another man, a rich farmer, whose biography the Master has outlined. He was the owner of rich and fertile fields, and in his community was looked upon as a prosperous and happy man. As men go, he was fully up to the average ; to be sure he is seldom found in the synagogue, but no great crimes can be laid at his door. Men look and say : "Prosperous, happy, successful man." But God looks down and sees and speaks : "Thou fool." That is a short biography, but it is full of profound significance ; it teaches more than many a three-volume memorial. One day, in the little town of Dothan, the servant of the prophet Elisha arose and went forth from the city. Soon he came running back in terror to his master, crying, "Alas, my master, what shall we do ? The city is compassed with horses and chariots." The young man saw the life of the man of God from the human side only, and he was afraid. But at the prayer of Elisha his eyes are opened, and behold, the mountains were full of horses and chariots of fire round about the prophet.

Here is this great busy human world, with its engrossments, its standards, its estimates of men and things, its honors and dishonors. Can we know how to separate the true from the false, the real from the apparent; how shall we know what to refuse and what to receive, what is the worthful and what is the worthless ? By the right use of the Scriptures we may gain this all-important power, and may know what is the verdict upon our lives in the courts of heaven. These men of Scripture whose lives are recorded are types of all men in all ages and lands. They give us the key to the interpretation of human life with all its problems and changes. The poet had learned this lesson when he wrote the striking lines :

> When God shall call the muster roll,
>   As heroes he'll mark off
> Some who ne'er charged at Waterloo,
>   Or stormed the Malakoff.
>
> Stars, garters, crosses, ribbons fade ;
>   New orders here unfold ;
> The widow's mite, St. Martin's cloak,
>   The cup of water cold.
>
> The hearts that saved the world by love,
>   And hourly Calvaries bore,
> The mother-martyrs, queenly host,
>   Are marshalled to the fore.
>
> Earth's black-robed throngs are clad in white;
>   Their brows a light adorns—
> A radiance of diamond,
>   Crowns of transfigured thorns.

> Some humble folk we knew quite well,
>   But passed with scarce a nod,
> Now rank as heaven's nobility,
>   The chivalry of God.
>
> Imperial names of history
>   Omitted from the list;
> In Paradise, preferment shows
>   A hidden satirist.
>
> GEORGE ALWAY.

The things recorded in Scripture, the Apostle tells us, are ensamples, and they are written down for our admonition. The Scriptures are given us that we may know what manner of men we are, and may know what is the verdict of heaven upon our lives.

4. And the Scriptures give us the key to our human experiences, and everyday doings. The heart of man is a great, restless, hungry ocean. Nothing that he has seen or handled has satisfied him. He is a great bundle of longings, discontents, aspirations, hopes, fears. Make him a councilman and he wants to be mayor; send him to Congress and he burns to be president. Give him half the world, and before night he will be wanting some field over in the other half. What is the meaning of this universal heart hunger? Scripture gives us the explanation. Our souls are athirst for God, for the living God. Augustine had entered into the truth of Scripture when he cried: "Thou hast made us for thyself, and our heart is restless till it find rest in thee." In the light of Scripture

we look across the world, and we see man longing for God, and God seeking for man.

We look over the world, and everywhere we are met with the sight of suffering, poverty, wretchedness and sin. Evils of all kinds abound; wrong often appears to be triumphant, while right languishes or goes to the wall. The whole world seems to lie in the power of the wicked one. They that be against man seem to be more and mightier than they that be for him. The outlook for man and for the race seems hopeless enough. But we change our observation point; we look out upon the world in the light of Scripture. Now all is changed. The great world is seen to lie in the light and love of the eternal God. Beyond our little systems, beyond the reach of our thought sweeps the great, loving purpose of God which none can change and none can thwart. Light is pushing back the darkness; right is crowding wrong over the frontier. The eternal God is man's refuge, and underneath are the everlasting arms. And there upon the shore of the sea stands the winning Christ who is drawing all men unto himself.

The standards of time and the standards of eternity are quite different. Not until a man has been measured by the eternal standards do we have his true rating in God's universe. Before going to sea, the ship captain is careful to regulate and set the chronometer. A few seconds variation on the stormy night may mean utter shipwreck.

Most important is it that men sailing the sea of life, that sea with so many contrary winds and dangerous reefs, with its eternally divergent harbors, should have some chart of the sea, some regulator of his course. Men need to know what manner of beings they are; they need to have some court of appeal for conscience, some text book of the inner life.

5. There is a disposition to banish God from the present, and to relegate him to some age and place far away. Men are quite ready to believe in a God once active in the world, and once interested in man. But to many men God has either been dead, or asleep, or on a journey for many centuries. At any rate they do not have a vital belief in a living God who is now present in the world, and active in behalf of man. We are all too much inclined to banish God to some other age or place; to locate him beyond the stars in the abysses of space; we do not expect to find him in our streets and in our homes in this dull and commonplace present. Men look back with longing to those happy early days when God came down to walk in the garden in the cool of the day, to talk with men. Oh, those happy, happy days, when the very air was quivering with the presence of God, when his voice was heard and his hand was felt. But now men speak as if God had left the plain on which they dwell and toil, and had gone up to the hills far out of sight and hearing of the children of men. We believe in the God of Abraham, Isaac

and Jacob; the God of David and Isaiah, of Peter and John; but we do not more than half believe in the ever-living, ever-present God.

There is no warrant in Scripture or in reason for drawing a circle around any age or place, and limiting God's presence and power to that little area. To shut God out of any age is to shut him out of all ages; to find him in any age is to find him in every age. The infinite God is infinitely at work in every part of his universe, at every moment of time. The Bible takes on a new meaning, and becomes a new book, when it becomes the regulator and type of God's continuous presence with his people, and his active interest in their behalf. The things that are recorded in the Scriptures are to be treated as types and symbols of what God is ever doing; its special incidents are the key to the interpretation of our own experiences. The very worst use of the Scriptures is to make us distrustful of our own deepest experiences of God. That disciple has not learned to use the Scriptures, who does not find in them the key to his own experiences and the norm of his own thought. For the Bible suggests far more than it directly reveals. The amount of explicit information it contains is small; the truth to which it directs us is infinite. It tells us where the rich treasure lodes are to be found; but it has not exhausted any of these mines. It tells us where to look for treasure, and how to interpret what we find; but it sends each soul direct to God, the fountain of all light and truth. The lowest possible use of the Scriptures is that which regards them as a body of statements to be learned by heart and repeated by rote. It is not the truth without us which makes us free, but the truth within us. It is not the Christ who once walked among men who is the hope of glory, but the Christ within us. The one great purpose of the Scriptures is to bring God and man together. They show us how to find God, how to recognize his presence, and how to live in him. A life lived according to Scripture models is sure to be a right life: a life lived apart from Scripture models and examples is quite sure to be defective in many important particulars.

II. IT MAY BE WORTH WHILE TO CONSIDER HOW TO STUDY THE SCRIPTURES FOR THE LARGEST PROFIT.

1. The Bible is to be studied by books for revelation. The Bible is a book, and it is also a collection of books. These various books are all gathered up and combined in the great purpose of God: each book is like a stone in the wall of a building: take away one stone, and the wall is weakened and the building is marred. But each book is in a sense complete in itself: it has its own revelation, its own purpose, its own lessons. One cannot be said to know his Bible, till he knows the setting of each book and the purpose of each writer.

Suppose we consider one of the books of the Bible. Several questions most naturally rise to our lips: who was the writer? To whom is he writing? what were the conditions under which he wrote? what were the great truths which he sought to present? One illustration from the Old Testament and one from the New will show the importance of these questions. We take the book of the prophet Hosea first. Turning to his book and reading carefully between the lines, we find a most sad and tragic story of domestic sorrow. He has married the beautiful Gomer, hoping no doubt, that the love of a pure and true man might win her away from the evil tendencies of her youth. But from the first she seems to have been faithless to him. Finally, she leaves him, and gives herself up to a life of profligacy and sin. Lower and lower she sinks, till at last she is cast off by the men with whom she has sinned, and is now exposed for sale as a common slave in the market-place. Hosea hears of it, and goes to the market-place to buy her. He takes her home, and cares for her, hoping no doubt that in the atmosphere of love and care a better mind might come to her. As he sits beside his desolate hearth, and draws his motherless boys to his heart, he ponders his sad experience. Now up through his poor human heart he looks and reads the heart of Jehovah. He sees how Jehovah has chosen, espoused Israel for himself: but, alas, Israel has proved faithless and perverse. The people forsake Jehovah for the foul and false gods of the nations. But he does not cast them off; his love endures through all their faithlessness. Though broken and reduced low, the people shall yet be brought back, and once more Jehovah shall rejoice over them. His book we find is addressed to an Israel faithless to a covenant relation, a nation guilty of the most black and graceless sins against love. For her sins Israel must be punished; but Jehovah has not cast them off forever, he is God and not man. The great truth he emphasizes is the love of Jehovah in choosing and espousing Israel for himself out of all the nations of the world, that they might be his own precious treasure. But from the first they were bent to backsliding, and from the first have been faithless to his covenant love. For their sins they must be punished; but in punishment he remembers mercy, and so gathers the broken remnant once more and cherishes them in a deathless love. To appreciate the wondrous beauty of the book and to enter into its great truths it must be studied in its entirety. By so doing one will gain some great truth about God.

Suppose we take the Gospel of Luke in the New Testament. We find that its author is an early disciple, who writes a letter to a friend, presumably a disciple also, and from his name undoubtedly a Greek. Other narratives claiming to be trustworthy accounts of the life of Jesus the Christ are in circulation, but these are not in all respects satisfactory. That Theophilus might know the certainty concerning the things wherein he has been instructed, this man takes his pen in hand

and frames a narrative. The writer wants this Greek to know that Jesus is the Friend of man; that his gospel is for all men both Jews and Greeks. So he embodies in his narrative many incidents in Christ's life that show his universal sympathy and world-wide interest. The book has a purpose definite and distinct; the incidents and teachings selected are not taken at haphazard, but are chosen to illustrate the author's purpose. The book must be taken as a whole, in order to comprehend the full purpose of the writer.

Such a course of study as is here indicated means work; but it is only the student who can enter into the deeper and richer treasures of Scripture. When the ruling thought, the dominant truth of each book is well in mind, let the student collect his materials. He will find that the lesson of each book finds its place in the growing process of God's self-revelation of himself to men. His sense of the God-inspired nature of the sacred writings will be increased tenfold. He will find also that the four Gospels, each so distinct and definite in its purpose, present a necessary aspect of that marvelous life. He will find that each supplements the other, and each is necessary to the complete picture. The disciple who wants to know his Bible must know it by books. Until he knows it in this way he does not know it as he ought to know it. Comparison of text with text for doctrine comes later. The student does not know how to use any text till he knows it in its relations and circumstances. The character that is to be formed and maintained on Bible principles must have its foundations laid deep and firm in an intelligent knowledge of the Scriptures.

2. The Bible is to be studied by characters for inspiration. The Bible is a revelation to men; but it is also, first of all, a revelation in men. The men of God of old, who were moved by the Holy Spirit, found God in their own truest and deepest experiences. The truth which these men give forth to the world has first lived within them in their own heart's experience of God. This makes the Bible such a real and human book, so true to the every-day experiences of men. The men of Scripture record were men of like passions with ourselves, men hoping and fearing, sinning and repenting, aspiring and fainting, sometimes certain of God, and sometimes losing him. The written word comes throbbing warm out of the inmost heart of the man. Just so far as we appreciate the reality of these men of Scripture, do we become sensible of the reality of God himself. To many people we fear these persons of Scripture are little else than painted figures, lay figures, mere penmen of the Holy Spirit, who tell of a hope they never knew, and record an experience they never felt. The Bible is an unreal, remote, mysterious book to many persons, for the very reason that they have never felt the intense reality and humanness of the lives recorded and the experiences told. Coleridge has voiced in vigorous

words a protest against this unreal way of conceiving Scripture characters and experiences. "Let me once be persuaded that all these heart-awakening utterances of human hearts—of men of like faculties and passions with myself, mourning, rejoicing, suffering, triumphing—are but as a *Divina Commedia* of a superhuman—O bear with me if I say it—Ventriloquist; that the royal Harper, to whom I have so often submitted myself as a many-stringed instrument for his fire-tipt fingers to traverse, while every several nerve of emotion, passion, thought, that thrills the flesh-and-blood of our common humanity, responded to the touch —that this sweet Psalmist was himself as mere an instrument as his harp, an automaton poet, mourner and supplicant—all is gone—all sympathy, at least, and all example. I listen in awe and fear, but likewise in perplexity and confusion of spirit" (Confessions of an Inquiring Spirit, Letter III.).

It is an old saying that grace does not find men saints, but makes them saints. The Scriptures have such surpassing value and such eternal interest, because they show us this saint-making in process. We see such a man as Jacob, the wily trickster, the supplanting deceiver, taken hold of by God's Spirit, and led along the way till he becomes Israel the prince of God. We see how, in the furnace of trial, God humbles him and chastens him, burning out the dross, and burning in holiness. We see how God takes the shapeless and dead lump of clay and fashions it up into a vessel of great usefulness and surpassing beauty.

No study can be more profitable and inspiring than the study of Scripture biographies. Carlyle used to say that there is no history, only biography; that history is at bottom made up of innumerable biographies. Nay, he says, is not the gospel itself but a surpassing biography? To know what man has felt and done in this world, to know what things help and what things hinder him, to see how God's grace comes into unlikeliest hearts, and makes all things new, to see how God chooses unpromising men and fits them for great services; to know also the rocks on which souls have made shipwreck of faith, and to know how to distinguish the eternal pole star from a wandering will-o'-wisp;—than this there can be no knowledge more important. To enjoy this use of the Bible one must study the great lives recorded there from beginning to end; one must understand the times in which they lived, and the circumstances against which they battled. One must study the life till he sees the world in which the man played his part, and enters that world with him, walking with him, communing with him, becoming his companion and friend. From the petty cares of the hour and from the crowd of unsympathetic companions one can then transport himself at will into the company of the best and greatest souls of earth, "where the brow of every one is crowned with nobleness, every eye beams encouragement, and the air is redolent of faith and hope and love."

3. And finally, the Bible is to be studied by topics for doctrine. We are living in an age that has become somewhat impatient of doctrine. Perhaps some of this impatience is not without reason, as doctrine has at times been emphasized rather than life. Great injustice has been done the Bible by those who have made it a storehouse of proof texts. Passages have been torn, throbbing and bleeding, out of their connection, and have been built into the cold and corpse-like form of some doctrine. Doctrine, after all that has been said, has its place in every first-rate life. Its place is at the foundation, and not at the capstone, of character. We are Christians, not that we may have right doctrines; but we need right doctrines that we may be strong Christians.

The apostle Paul is one of the most doctrinal writers of the Bible, and he is one of the most practical. Everything depends upon the reader's point of view. In almost every one of his epistles he begins with setting forth some great and far-reaching truth about God and man, sin and redemption. He lays the foundations of the Christian life deep in the eternal truths of God. He wants believers to be rooted and grounded in the truth as it is in Christ Jesus. Upon this foundation he then builds the structure of a full-rounded Christian practice. With him doctrine builds itself up into life. On the other hand, he wants every practical duty to have deep and strong foundations. The most commonplace and ordinary duties of life he builds upon the solid and enduring truths of God. It is not fashionable in these days to admire the Puritans and their doctrines. No doubt their doctrines were often hard and narrow and rigid: but those doctrines put iron into men's blood, and made strong men, strong to endure, and brave for God. The writer of the epistle to the Hebrews had scant patience with those Christians who were content to remain forever in the spoon-victual stage of development. He wants men to leave the first principles of the doctrine of Christ, the simple elementary duties of life, and pass on and up into manhood, where they may partake of the solid and strong meat of the word.

In the Scriptures a few great doctrines or topics stand out conspicuous and important. Of course, truth is one thing and the doctrine of the truth is quite another. God, Christ, the Holy Spirit, sin, redemption, immortality and judgment are great realities. To attempt to put these great realities into a doctrine seems almost like attempting to convey the aroma of the rose in a formula, or to paint a sunset with only one color. But right thought goes before right action. So every man who wants to build up a strong and enduring character will build upon the great doctrines of the Scriptures. He will learn to study his Bible by topics, and gradually he will find that a body of doctrine is building itself up in his mind, and is determining his thinking in all realms and on all questions. "Omnia exeunt in theologiam." Men are too easily satisfied with taking isolated texts and dwelling on them. So few are willing to undergo the toil necessary to compass the Bible as a whole. Most important is it, that he who would know his Bible should go through the whole Bible to find out just what is taught there on the great questions of life and destiny. Why should not the Christian who seeks to be strong in faith and conduct make an attempt to grasp the great fundamental truths of the Bible, for the sake of faith on the one hand, and for the sake of conduct on the other? Paul commends Timothy, because from a child he has known the Holy Scriptures, which are able to make thee wise unto salvation, through faith in Christ Jesus. He says also that Scripture "is profitable for reproof, for correction, for instruction in righteousness, that the man of God may be perfect thoroughly furnished unto all good works."

CHAPTER III.

THE ROAD OVER CALVARY.

> I have been crucified with Christ; yet I live; and yet no longer I, but Christ liveth in me.—THE APOSTLE PAUL.
>
> Behold! in the cross all doth consist, and all lieth in our dying thereon; for there is no other way unto life, and unto true inward peace but by the way of the holy cross, and of daily mortification.
>
> If thou bear the cross cheerfully it will bear thee, and lead thee to the desired end, namely, where there shall be an end of suffering though here there shall not be.
>
> If thou bear it unwillingly, thou makest for thyself a burden, and increasest thy load, which yet notwithstanding thou must bear.—THOMAS à KEMPIS.
>
> The cross of Christ avails thee nothing till it is erected in thine own life also.—*A German Mystic.*

INTO the hands of Bunyan's Pilgrim, there has come a book which greatly interests him. This book he opens and reads; and as he reads he trembles and weeps. At last in bitterness of soul he cries out, "What shall I do?" While in this troubled state he meets Evangelist, who points across a wide field to a wicket gate and advises Christian to enter there. Various false advisers for a time divert Pilgrim from his purpose; but their advice brings him no peace; rather shame and misery. The great burden which he has been carrying becomes heavier and heavier, till he is almost crushed beneath it. Once more, on the counsel of Evangelist, he pursues his way and comes to the house of Interpreter. Here many things are made plain to the inquirer, who now sets his face resolutely toward the Celestial City. He is shown a highway, fenced in on either side with a wall, and that wall is called Salvation. Up this way the Pilgrim runs, but with great difficulty, on account of the heavy load upon his back. Soon along this climbing way he comes in sight of a cross upon a hill, and below in the valley a sepulchre. "So I saw in my dream that just as Christian came up with the cross his burden loosed from off his shoulders and fell from off his back, and began to tumble, and so continued to do till it came to the mouth of the sepulchre, where it fell in, and I saw it no more." Three Shining Ones salute him; the first pronounces words of forgiveness; the second clothes him in bright new raiment; and the third sets a mark upon his forehead, and gives him a roll. Then Christian gave three leaps for joy, and went on his way singing with glad and hopeful heart.

The Christian who would enter into the new life of God finds that his way leads over Calvary. At the foot of Christ's cross he lays down his burden of guilt and shame, and takes up a song of joy and peace. Through the blood of the cross he is delivered from the power and penalty of sin, and is brought near to God. But the cross is more than a fact once met, an experience once known. As the seeker after life, on his way, he bears with him more than the experience of a fact or the memory of an experience. The cross once a fact which brought peace and hope, now becomes a daily experience and a law of life. The Christian thinks of Christ's cross, and finds deliverance and life through it. The Lord Jesus speaks of the disciple's cross, and calls upon the Christian to take up that cross and bear it daily. In a word, the disciple knows the cross as a fact and bears it daily as an experience. The Christian doctrine of the cross makes that cross at once the means of salvation and the law of life for man. These two aspects of the cross let us now consider in their bearing upon the life and character of the Christian disciple. No attempt is made to explain the theological doctrine of the atonement; my purpose is to show the bearing of this truth upon Christian life and character.

I. The Cross of Christ is the Means of our Redemption from the Power and Penalty of Sin.

Three things are wrought by the cross. It reveals God to the world; it delivers man from sin; and by it God and man are brought together.

1. The cross reveals God to the world. Back of the cross of Christ is the deepest fact of the universe. This world of ours was framed to bear a cross. The cross of wood laid upon the shoulders of the Son of man is but the shadow of that older cross which the Son of God bore upon his

heart from all eternity. The Lamb slain outside the city gates was the Lamb slain from the foundation of the world. He who walked the streets of Nazareth and Capernaum, who agonized in the garden and toiled up Calvary, was set apart for that work before the morning stars sang together. Jesus Christ, the Lamb slain from the foundation of the world, is the beginning of the creation of God. In fact, Jesus Christ is the author and medium of creation. The Son of God was in the world long before his manifestation as the Son of man. Very plain is the statement, "In him were all things created, in the heavens and upon the earth, things visible and things invisible, whether thrones, or dominions or principalities, or powers; all things have been created through him, and unto him; and he is before all things, and in him all things consist" (Col. i. 16, 17). When we speak of Christ coming into the world we do not mean that then and there in that historic event we call the incarnation, those relations began in the Godhead which we know as Father and Son. We only mean that in that historic event these eternal relations are manifested to the world.

The whole creation is God's self-manifestation in Jesus Christ as love and holiness. Why God should have chosen to create such a world as this, with such sinful and painful possibilities, let us say frankly we do not know. We know, however, because we know that God is good, that it is not only the best possible universe, but the only possible universe for the object God has in view. Why God should create a universe subject to the bondage of corruption, and thus impose upon himself the necessity of sacrifice, we do not know. After all, when does God appear most divine? When does his glory shine out most brightly? Is it when angels bow and seraphim veil their faces? No, no; but when he gives himself for his creatures. We say that a mother loves her children; what do we mean by the words? And when does the mother show most love for her children; when is she most the mother? Is it when the children gather around her knee to look their love and gratitude into her eyes? That is indeed a beautiful sight; but not in this way can we know the depths and heights of a mother's love. But see her now with sleepless eye and tireless hand watching day and night beside her sick and suffering child. Or see her as she sets the light in the window to welcome her prodigal daughter home. Or, see her as she goes out after her wayward boy, following him to his haunts of sin, and pleading with him to leave these evil ways. God is never so truly and fully God as when he sacrifices and suffers for his needy creatures. Revelation has been given to make us see that God is love and holiness. Love can only be shown in all its fullness in the presence of things that hurt and wound love. Holiness can only be revealed in its inner nature in a deathless passion for truth and righteousness. Suppose, for a moment, that God had never created this world at all. Suppose that this world had not been made subject to vanity and corruption. Calvary had then been without its cross, and the Son of God without his wounds. But we say it reverently, the universe had been unspeakably, immeasurably poorer. We never would have known the interior nature of God; we would never have known the meaning of love and holiness. And it is true, as Browning says:

> "The loving worm within its clod
> Were diviner far than a loveless God,
> Amid his worlds, I will dare to say."

But in Jesus Christ, God manifest in the flesh, in his acceptance of the cross and his sacrifice for man, the universe has had a glimpse into the very heart of God. Through the cross of Calvary there has come to the universe a revelation of God so full, so glorious, as to make all conscious beings taste the ecstacy and beauty of the inner knowledge of God.

The cross of Jesus Christ reveals God as love and holiness. And these are final truths about God. Men have sometimes spoken as if they found in Christ qualities that were not to be found in God. They have spoken as if they feared that the Son of man were more loving and compassionate than the eternal Father. But the love and self-sacrifice of Christ were the love and self-sacrifice of God. The cross shows us God himself bearing the sins of the world upon his heart, and sacrificing himself for the good of his creatures. Love, by the very nature of the case, seeks the good of the one loved, and is willing to make any sacrifices for the other's sake. Love says : "Let me share your burden; let me bear pain that you may escape." God is love, says John, as if love were a final and elemental fact of Godhead ; and it is. Love is the very essence of his being; it lies at the root of all his attributes ; it shines out in all his dealings with the children of men. The sunbeam strikes a rain drop and we have the seven colors of the rainbow. But the seven rays are all elements of the one blessed light. Love gives great hostages. Pain is inseparable from love.

> "Oh, the hurt, the hurt of love !
> Wherever the sun shines, the waters go,
> It hurts the snowdrop, it hurts the dove,
> God on his throne, and man below."

Would a man know how great is the love of God for sinful men ? Would he know how great is God's passion for holiness ? Would he know how infinitely he hates sin ? Would he know how urgent is his demand for righteousness ? Let him look upon the cross of Christ and he shall know. To see and believe the love of God is the first step toward salvation. To know God and Jesus Christ whom he has sent is eternal life.

2. The cross brings deliverance to man from the dominion of sin. The cross is such a potent thing because of its power to loose men from their sins

and to give them hope. "Sin well discovered to a man." said good Archbishop Leighton, "is half cured." The cross of Christ shows the moral condition of the world as nothing else can. "Sin," we are told, is the "transgression of the law." Yes, but it is the law of God ; and law is the expression of his being. Sin, in the last analysis, is an offence against God ; it is hatred of the light ; it is the child refusing the will of the father. The law given through Moses had done much to convince the world of sin ; but the cross of Christ does more. We never knew what sin was till we saw it crucifying the Son of God. Around the cross surges that mocking, taunting, hooting crowd, reviling the sufferer, spitting in his face, and laughing at his agony. What has he done that he should be thus hated, and taunted, and scourged ? Nothing ; men are hating him without a cause, and mocking him without a reason. The world's treatment of Jesus Christ is simply the full expression of the sin in the heart of man. This One who hangs upon the cross was full of grace and truth ; he went about doing good, comforting the sorrowing, seeking the outcast, cheering the discouraged, counselling the wayward, telling men of the Father in heaven. We might suppose that every man would at once love this Christ and honor his life. Among them walked Incarnate Goodness and Love ; before them stood Perfect Truth and Life. You know what men did with this Christ, the very life and love of God ; they refused him, they ridiculed him, they hated him, they adjudged him guilty of blasphemy, they sent him to the cross as a malefactor. By so doing they have put upon record forever this fact: the human heart is enmity against God and is far gone from the way of his holiness. Sin is not an innocent, harmless thing; it is hatred of the light; it is hatred of the good; it is night refusing the sun; it is a blow at God's throne. It was sin that sent Jesus Christ to the cross, my sin, your sin. Sin is the same thing in me as sin in the Pharisee. The sin in Caiaphas and the sin in you springs from the same taproot: it is all of one piece. The forms of manifestations of sin may be different in different men, but its real nature is the same. The cross rebukes our selfishness, our frivolity, our carnality, our petty aims, our unworthy deeds, our sinful hearts. Oh, the power of that cross to convince men of sin! How it burns with the holiness of God! How the sight of that cross burns the conviction of sin deep into the heart and conscience of man!

But if the power of the cross stopped here, it would fail us at the most vital point. Along with this there comes through the cross a deliverance from the power of sin over the heart and life. We look upon the cross of Christ, and we read there the infinite love of God for men. We see in the agony of the dying Saviour how the heart of the Eternal Father yearns over us with an infinite compassion. And we see also how our sins nailed him to that tree; how he takes upon himself our guilt; how he is wounded for our iniquities; how the chastisement of our peace is upon him. We see him by the grace of God tasting death for every man, and being made sin for us, this One who knew no sin. Against the thunders of Sinai we knew how to dull our ears; under the rebukes of God we knew how to harden our hearts. But there, beside the cross, the love looking forth from the Saviour's eyes speaks right home to our hearts. What the law could not do, in that it was weak, the cross has done. We see ourselves just as we are; we abhor ourselves for our sins; the flood gates of the soul are opened, and the tears of repentance flow. We fall at the pierced feet and cry: "Lord be merciful to me, a sinner." No one can put this truth better than it has been put by good John Newton in that matchless hymn:—

> " I saw One hanging on a tree,
>   In agony and blood;
> Who fixed his languid eyes on me,
>   As near the cross I stood.
>
> " Sure, never, till my latest breath,
>   Can I forget that look;
> It seemed to charge me with his death,
>   Though not a word he spoke.
>
> " Alas, I know not what I did—
>   But now my tears are vain;
> Where shall my trembling soul be hid?
>   For I the Lord have slain!

> "A second look he gave, that said :
> "I freely all forgive ;
> This blood is for thy ransom paid ;
> I die that thou mayst live."

> "Thus, while his death my sin displays,
> In all its blackest hue ;
> Such is the mystery of grace,
> It seals my pardon, too !"

At the sight of the cross we see our sin, and in sincere repentance we put it away. And the chains of sin drop off from our emancipated soul, and we rise up the Lord's free man. Our affections are given a new direction ; our wills are renewed ; and we are new men in Christ Jesus. The dominion of sin over the life is broken, a new master of our will appears, the conscience is purged from dead works to serve the living God.

3. And the cross brings God and man together. The work of Christ for man sums itself up in this reconciliation of God and man. God is the high and holy One, who cannot look upon sin with the least degree of allowance ; man is by act and choice a sinner. To bring God and man together on terms of fellowship and peace is the work of Jesus Christ in the world. God cannot overlook sin nor treat it indifferently. He cannot bless the soul so long as it continues in sin.

Suppose that a man who has been living in sin at last comes to see the error and folly of his way ; suppose also that he resolves to change his course and do differently. Has everything been done that needs to be done ? Has he fully satisfied every claim upon his life ? By no means. The mere resolve to leave one way and to walk in another does not bring peace to the troubled conscience. For we are not alone in this transaction : "There is another factor in this problem greater than I. I have done more than wrong myself. As a creature I have wronged my Creator. I have sinned against the laws ordained by him for the health and comfort of my body. I have sinned against the image of God in my soul, putting it to shame in this subjection to bestial appetite ; and I cannot look God in the face. I have no right to forgive myself. I cannot forgive myself. God would have to die first. Eternity would have to end first" (Roswell D. Hitchcock : Eternal Atonement, p. 20). Before man can be at peace, satisfaction must be rendered to the law of God which has been violated. The righteous will of God must be honored ; and man must come into right relations with that law. Three elements enter into this experience of reconciliation. There is the repentant one turning unto God and putting away his sin ; on the part of God there is the Fatherly acceptance and pardon of the soul ; there is the mutual relation that follows in which there is an imparting by God and a receiving by man of grace and power by which God and man live together in vital fellowship. Thus the man who once lived in sin, being dead unto God, by nature the child of wrath, is quickened by grace, brought near by Christ and reconciled unto God by the blood of the cross. This union with God through Jesus Christ is salvation. Express it as men will, the cross stands for the greatest fact in life ; before that cross the burden of sin is loosed from off man's shoulders ; through that cross man is reconciled unto God ; in that cross the covenant of God and man is sealed.

II. The Cross is the Disciple's Law of Life.

1. The being of God which finds expression in the sacrifice of Jesus Christ is the law of life for every creature. The being of God is the law of the universe. And sacrificial love is the deepest fact of Godhead. God cannot have one law for himself and another for his creatures. The Lamb slain from the foundation of the world shows us that sacrificial love is the law of the very throne of God. This law Christ honors in his life and death and establishes as the law of life for every creature. The necessity of the cross is upon everything that God has made. The cross is more than an historic fact; it is the expression of the law of the universe. The Lord Jesus has laid down the condition of discipleship : "If any man would come after me, let him deny himself, and take up his cross daily, and follow me." Another time he said to the disciples : "As my Father hath sent me into the world, even so send I you." That law which Jesus honors in his life and death he establishes as the law of life for every disciple.

The disciple is not greater than his Lord. Every man who would live in Jesus Christ must take up his cross, bear it out to Calvary, and die upon it. The cross of Christ is not a substitute for the cross of the disciple; it is the type, the pattern, the power of that cross which every disciple is to bear for the sake of the world. The real Christian life is a repetition of Christ's life. This human meaning of the cross has been almost overlooked in the life and thought of men. Men have thought of Christ's cross and have rested in it; Christ thinks of our cross, and calls upon us to take it up and follow him out to Calvary. The cross of Christ has profited a man nothing until it has been erected in his own heart as the law of life.

> "Though Christ a thousand times,
> In Bethlehem be born;
> If he's not born in thee,
> Thy soul is still forlorn;
> The cross of Golgotha
> Can never save thy soul,—
> The cross in thine own heart
> Alone can make thee whole."

The New Testament writings are full of this great truth. Paul affirms that he is crucified with Christ; he speaks of himself as a partner in the sufferings of Christ; he tells us that the old man is crucified with Christ that the body of sin might be destroyed. Writing to the Corinthians he speaks once more of himself as one who always bears about in his body the dying of the Lord

Jesus. John tells us that in this we perceive the love of God for us, because he laid down his life for us; and he makes this the reason why we should lay down our lives for others. It is easy, of course, to say that these are but figures of speech; but that is just what they are not. No; they stand for the most real and literal experiences of life. We have no more right to explain them away as figurative than we have to make the cross of Christ a figure of speech. These words mean that just as Christ Jesus honored the law of God in his life and gave himself in sacrifice for us, so we are to honor that law, and to give our lives in sacrifice for others. We are saved through the sacrifice of Christ; now we are to go out into the world of sinful men and offer ourselves in sacrifice for them that they may know God and Jesus Christ whom he has sent. Jesus Christ had the same call to bear the cross that every disciple has; and no other. Surely if any one had a right to the palace and the feast, to the life of ease and honor, it was the Lord Jesus, the Son of God's love. "But even Christ pleased not himself." The necessity of the cross was upon him.

2. Discipleship always and everywhere means exactly the same thing. You and I must face the same conditions that faced men in Capernaum, in Corinth, Ephesus, or Rome. The needle's eye has grown no larger in the passing centuries. Whoever would follow Christ to the throne must deny himself, take up his cross, and become a

partner in Christ's sacrifice. He in whose life there is no Calvary, no self is crucified and God's will not honored, knows not the inner meaning and divine power of the Christian life. Many people live in the delusion that the cross of Christ is a substitute for any cross on their part. But the self-denying, self-sacrificing life is the only kind of life that any man has a moral right and a divine warrant to live in this world of sin and suffering. The disciple is called to fill up in his body the measure of the sufferings of Christ; he is to repeat forever the sacrifice of Calvary; he is to be crucified with Christ. To many people, I know, this old simple truth of the gospel comes as some new and strange doctrine. But it is the very essence of the cross of Christ; it is the truth that has been preached from the beginning. And this is a truth that needs to be burned deep into the heart and consciences of men to-day. For alas, the cross in its real meaning has become an offense to many who hope to be saved by it. Not yet has the offense of the cross ceased. Many people do not like this gospel of the cross; they prefer some easier road to glory; they are quite willing to hear of Christ's cross, but they do not want to hear of their own cross. The cross is the law by which Jesus lived, and it is the law by which he asks his disciple to live. The cross is therefore not life's burden and accident, but life's law and glory. Remember the word of the Lord Jesus, how he said : " It is more blessed to give than to receive." Do you suppose that Jesus taught that without first doing it himself? Do you suppose that God put that impulse into the heart of Christ, but himself finds it more blessed to receive than to give? The necessity of the cross is upon every creature. As Christians we have the same right to please ourselves, to spend money as we like, to eat what we choose, to live in a palace, that Christ had; and no other right than he. As Christians we shall find our blessedness where Jesus found his—in honoring the law of God and in giving himself for others; and we shall find it nowhere else. The cross was no figure of speech to the Lord Jesus; and it is no figure of speech to the Christian disciple. How many lives can be told in these words:

> " I lived for myself, I thought for myself,
> For myself, and none beside;
> Just as if Jesus had never lived—
> As if he had never died."

The Christian is Christ continued—the divine incarnation made permanent, increased, carried along; the cross of Christ is the type and power and expression of that sacrifice which every creature is called to make. Through the cross of Christ we are delivered from the old bondage of sin and self, and are reconciled to the person and will of God. We are brought into union with Jesus Christ, that we may live his life. Jesus Christ cannot have one law for himself and another law for his disciples. He has given us an example that we should do as he has done.

3. The cross of Jesus Christ teaches us that we are to organize life on the basis of love and sacrifice. The law of the cross is the only law which the throne of God honors. If any man is not willing to deny himself, take up his cross daily and follow Christ, he is none of his. And the law of the cross is universal in its sweep and all-inclusive in its requirement. The necessity of the cross is upon everything that God has made. The law of the cross is the law for men, for societies, for churches, for stock exchanges, for railroad companies, for political parties, for halls of legislation, for international treaties. This law, it is hardly necessary to say, is not generally accepted to-day. Men have more or less applied it to their personal lives, to their churches, and to their families. But men have hardly begun to suspect that it is the law for the mill, the political party, and the railroad company. A railroad company has no more right to plan for dividends alone than a church or a family. A political party has no more liberty to forget the decalogue and the sermon on the mount than a missionary society. It is as bad to be selfish and mercenary in the store as in the house of prayer. The missionary has no greater call to live the sacrificial life than the merchant. The minister has no more urgent obligation to sink personal interests out of sight than the politician. Self-interest is the law which

Satan asserts in Cain; self-sacrifice is the law which God reveals in Christ. And the problem of every life, of every institution, of every nation is simply this: Shall Christ reign or Cain? The law of self-interest, which is the law of death, asks: Am I my brother's keeper? It says: Every man must look out for himself. Selfishness is the basis of economic activity. Competition is the law of industry. Life is a struggle for existence, and the strong survive. And right into this world comes Jesus Christ to assert another law, and by his cross to establish another principle of life. The old law of self-interest said: "Every man must look out for himself, and get all he can." The new law of God says: "Bear ye one another's burdens, and so fulfill the law of Christ." The old law of competition said: "Life is a battle for supremacy, and every man must take care of himself." The new law of Christ says: "Look not every man on his own things, but every man also on the things of others."

The Christian Citizen is in the world, but he is not of the world. He does not ask to be taken out of the world, but he asks rather that he may be kept from the evil of the world. He repudiates the law of Cain and accepts the law of Christ. He desires to follow Christ; so he denies himself, takes up his cross daily, and makes the cross the law of his life. He seeks to organize life in the home, in the state, in the church, in society, on the basis of the cross. He knows that nothing but the cross can save the world. Nothing but the cross can save society from dissolution and anarchy. Nothing but the blood of the cross can bind the race together in a solidarity of redemption and peace. The cross is God's answer to the problems of society. Let the citizen in his business relations resolve to reckon himself dead unto self and alive unto Christ; let him resolve to conduct all his commercial transactions according to the law of the cross. He may fail to make money; he may succeed in doing so. He is not here to make money, but to glorify Jesus Christ. Let the New Citizen in his political life reckon himself dead unto the standards of men who regard public office as a place of honor and praise, and let him make his political privilege an altar for the offering of spiritual sacrifices unto God. He may never be chosen to the highest offices; or he may become the hero of a nation; it does not matter either way. He is not here to gain position but to hold up the cross in the sight of all men. The cross is a real thing, a potent thing. Oh, believe that. Forever that cross, when erected, becomes the power of God unto salvation to men and to society. We cannot regenerate society by each man living for himself. We cannot reform politics by making a ring to break a ring. How can Satan cast out Satan? The cross is God's answer to our cry for help; the cross is God's way of saving the world: and there is no other. *And the cross will do it.*

Brother Citizen, do not turn back saying that the road is too hard and the cross too heavy. The most tragic mistake you can make is to suppose that the way of the cross is a hard and bitter road. Do you suppose that the law of the throne of God, the law which God honors, and Christ fulfills, and the cross establishes, is a hard and bitter thing? The Lord Jesus found it more blessed to give than to receive. Do you suppose that you will ever find it more blessed to receive than to give? The Son of man found it his meat and drink to do the will of the Father in heaven? Do you suppose that you will ever find it meat and drink to do your own will? The Son of God foresaw the cross and embraced it with joy, saying: "I delight to do thy will, O my God." Do you suppose that you will ever find it a blessed thing to escape that cross? Jesus Christ for the joy that was set before him, endured the cross and despised the shame. God is love; and love is God. Be sure of this, that the selfish, self-seeking life is not worth the living. The law of the cross, which was the law of life for the Lord Jesus, must be a blessed thing for every man, for every angel, for every world. The man who has once tasted the real meaning of the cross has tasted the very ecstasy of God. The will of God revealed in the cross of Christ is the best and brightest and sweetest thing for every creature. That cross is not life's burden, and accident, and sorrow, but life's joy, and glory, and crown. The cross, once well known in a man's life, in all its power and meaning, makes all lower things but dross for evermore.

CHAPTER IV.

THE INNER ROOM.

But thou, when thou prayest, enter into thy closet, and when thou hast shut thy door, pray to thy Father which is in secret; and thy Father which seeth in secret shall reward thee openly.—JESUS CHRIST.

Prayer is the spiritual balm which restores to us peace and courage. It reminds us of pardon and of duty. It says to us, Thou art loved—love; thou hast received—give; thou must die—labor while thou canst; overcome anger with kindness; overcome evil with good.—HENRI-FREDERIC AMIEL.

Prayer is the nearest approach to God, and the highest enjoyment of him that we are capable of in this life.

It is the noblest exercise of the soul, the most exalted use of our best faculties, and the highest imitation of the blessed inhabitants of heaven.—WILLIAM LAW.

SEVERAL years ago thinking men became impressed with the importance of preserving the Adirondack forests of the State of New York. Scientific men explained that the preservation of these forests was necessary in order to maintain the proper flow of water in the Hudson River, the great commercial highway of the state. This river in its course furnishes power to countless mills and factories, and adds incalculably to the wealth of the people. Yet this river is in danger of losing its power and prestige. Up among the hills and mountains are the great trees with their countless leaves that shade the ground and keep it moist and cool. On every hillside and in every valley are little bubbling springs; from each spring a narrow thread of silver goes sparkling down over stones and under moss; now it is met by another thread of silvery water; on they go together, lost in one another's life; now the thread grows into a rill, the rill becomes a brook, the brook swells into a creek, the creek widens out into the majestic and beautiful Hudson. The drying up of those numberless springs far away in the mountains means the dwindling of a great river. The mighty and majestic river has its sources far away in those little springs in shady nook and quiet valley. Dry up the springs, cut off the head waters, and the river will dwindle and narrow.

In Christian prayer we find the unseen sources of Christian character. The power shown in holy living is power gained in the closet. No Christian character can either be made or maintained without prayer. The New Citizen is called to live and serve in the city in the sight of all his fellows. But it is in The Inner Room that he learns to live and gains the strength to serve. God had one Son, who lived without sin, but he had no Son who lived without prayer. The only sinless life this world ever saw was the most prayerful life. Jesus Christ, Son of God, Son of man, could not get along without constant prayer. We read of him that, as his custom was, he went out to the mountain to pray; we read of his spending whole nights in prayer. Every new day of his life brought its new reasons for prayer. It was in prayer that the Holy Spirit came upon him; it was in prayer that he was transfigured; it was in prayer that the angel came to strengthen him; it was in prayer that he breathed out his soul upon the cross.

It may be worth while to consider the place of prayer in the making and maintaining of Christian character.

I. The Three Reasons for Prayer.—1. There is the reason of human need and weakness. Man, it has been said, is the only creature that naturally looks up; for all other beings the heavens have no attraction. It has been pointed out also, that the old Greek word for man signifies the upward looking one. Be this as it may, man is the only creature who is conscious of deep wants which only heaven can supply. Man is a great bundle of longings. He is by nature the unsatisfied, the aspiring, the needy one. The heart of man is a great, deep, hungry ocean which nothing can fill. All the rivers of a continent carry down their tribute of water; yet the sea never overflows. "When I was a boy," said Thackeray, "I wanted some taffy. It was a shilling; I hadn't one. When I was a man I had the shilling, but I didn't want the taffy." Hear these words of Thomas Carlyle: "Man's unhappiness, as I construe, comes of his greatness; it is because there is an

Infinite in him, which with all his cunning he cannot quite bury under the Finite. Will the whole Finance Ministers, and upholsterers and confectioners of modern Europe undertake, in joint stock company, to make one shoe-black happy? They cannot accomplish it above an hour or two; for the shoe-black also has a soul quite other than his stomach; and would require, if you consider it, for his permanent satisfaction and saturation, simply this allotment, no more, and no less; God's Infinite Universe altogether to himself, therein to enjoy infinitely, and fill every wish as fast as it rose." Set alongside this word of Carlyle the complemental truth of Augustine: "Thou hast made us for thyself, and our heart is restless until it find rest in thee." God is the Eternal One, and he has set eternity in the heart of man. Across the years of time and the wanderings of man deep calleth unto deep. Because man is a needy, dependent creature, made by God and made for God, he must pray.

Man's needs are as wide as his nature. He needs sympathy, and guidance, and forgiveness; he needs also a personal friend and companion and God. Man needs sympathy; he needs to know that the power above him is a personal and loving power. Science tells us that no two atoms in the universe touch one another. The atoms in a solid piece of steel are separated by a distance greater than their diameters. Life is full of surprises; all the time we are coming to chasms of distance that widen between ourselves and those we thought were living in touch with us. Soon or late every soul finds that in the very deepest experiences of life it is alone. But such loneliness is intolerable to man. So his heart cries out for God, the great companion, the one who is nearer to us than we are to ourselves.

"Speak to him, thou, for he hears, and spirit with spirit can meet;
Closer is he than breathing, and nearer than hands and feet."

Man needs help for life's battles and guidance along life's pathway. The man who knows most of himself is the one most ready to confess his own insufficiency. It is worth noting that the Scriptures nowhere enforce prayer as a duty. "To force it as a duty," said Robertson of Brighton, "is dangerous. Christ did not; never commanded it, never taught it till asked." The reason of this is plain: necessity makes its own obligation. Man needs instruction as to the objects of prayer, the condition and manner of prayer, but he does not need to have prayer in itself enforced as a duty. The man who does not pray is either ignorant of himself or ignorant of God. More and more the conviction forces itself upon one that beyond everything else men need help. And to whom shall men go for this help? Our fellows can help us with food and work, they can help us with advice and counsel. But every one has felt himself saying at times of all such efforts: "Miserable comforters are ye all." To whom shall the young man go when the blood of passion is running hot in his veins? To whom shall the mourning mother go when the shadow of God's hand passes over the home, and a chair is emptied? To whom shall the man go whose brain is all confused over the perplexities of life and the problems of destiny? Never to pray,—what does that mean? Never to be conscious of any need, never to aspire after God, never to look gratitude into the face of the eternal Father, never to lift up the eye unto God who guides us with his eye.

And man needs to pray that he may come into personal relations with the living God. The world that man sees bulks very large in his thought and interest. And this world he sees seems to be a world under the control of secondary causes. That is, law seems to reign throughout the universe, and man's life seems to be shut in by fixed and unalterable laws. He seems to be but a link "in an endless and aimless series of cosmical changes." Too often nature looks into his face as a great horrible death-mask, with no heart that loves, no will that lives behind it. No one has expressed this in more striking language than that prose poet, Jean Paul Richter, in his dream of a world without God. "And when I looked up to the boundless universe for the divine eye, behold, it glared at me from out a socket, empty, and bottomless. Over the face of chaos brooded Eternity chewing it forever, again and yet again." The heart of man was made for fellowship with the eternal Father. Man cannot rest content in a power that rules by law and fate; he craves a Person who loves, a will that rules, a Father who saves and guides.

2. Again: the second reason why man should pray is that in prayer God imparts his choicest gifts to the soul. We are encouraged in Scripture to bring to God our daily wants and troubles; we are encouraged to believe that he will give us the things that we ask at his hands. But it must ever be remembered that God's choicest gift to man is himself. Deeper than any prayer for anything that God has to give is the prayer for God himself to come into the life and dwell there. How few of the prayers of the Psalmist are for specific objects; how many of them are longings after God. The fact is prayer consummates itself in this deep and final longing after God. The highest blessing which God can make known unto man is himself. It is in prayer that God imparts himself to man, and man receives from God. The divine Father can do more in a praying man than in any other, for the reason that such a soul is more open and responsive to his grace and love. The Father gives himself without measure; but God can give no faster than man can receive. Prayer is the soul of man opening itself out to receive the inflowing grace of God. Men do not

become saints in their sleep; they do not receive the grace of God in fulness without their own co-operation. We do not enter upon the debated grounds of God's sovereignty and man's free agency. Whatever may be the case at the beginning of the Christian life, through life the condition obtains that man's willingness to receive conditions God's ability to give. It is neither by special Divine favor nor by happy human chance that certain men obtained nearness to God and fulness of his spirit. The great men of God in all ages have been men of great prayer. Few men enjoy the nearness to God enjoyed by Brainerd and Spurgeon, Samuel Rutherford and Martin Luther, for the simple reason that few men are willing to undergo the sweat of soul in prayer. Read this leaf out of the diary of David Brainerd: "Lord's Day, April 25th. This morning spent about two hours in sacred duties, and was enabled more than ordinarily to agonize for immortal souls; though it was early in the morning and the sun scarcely shone at all, yet my body was quite wet with sweat." Prayer is the soul of man opening itself to receive the life of God. And often this exercise of soul calls for a mighty effort of will, an effort which few men are willing to make. Man needs to pray because to the praying soul God comes, and in the praying soul he dwells.

3. And a third reason for prayer is that by prayer God's blessings are brought to men. A man's desires for himself are the measure of his desires for

all mankind. Prayer for others is a necessity to the soul that knows God. Many there are who make light of this aspect of prayer. There are those who say that as a spiritual exercise nothing can be more useful than prayer; but its objective efficacy is out of the question. Surely no one who accepts the supernatural origin of Christianity can deny that prayer exerts a power outside the soul of the petitioner. It may be well to notice the two classes of objections that are made to this outside efficacy of prayer. The objections come from two sources: from love and from law.

In the name of God's fatherly love some would tell us that prayer for any object outside our own personal lives is unnecessary. It is said that God loves all men, and seeks to bless and help them. No word of man's can ever make him more ready to bless and help. And he knows so much better than man what his children need, that any word of suggestion seems like a distrust of his love and wisdom. Does it not appear more becoming, more filial, such men say, to put a general trust in him, and to rest quietly in his providences? There is a truth here which can never be emphasized too strongly. God does love his people with an everlasting love, and he is more ready to give than they are to receive. But this argument, while it seems to foster trust, easily allows us to go on in our way and to leave God out of our lives. The object of prayer, let us say it, is not to inform God nor to change his will. But God has ordained prayer as the means through which his blessings flow out to men. God has, as the final purpose of our lives, the training of our souls to habits of personal intercourse and filial devotion. We are made for sonship; and sonship is personal co-operation, personal fellowship with God in his infinite impulse to bless mankind. Sonship is personal co-operation with him in the fulfillment of his plans in the world. Sonship is personal fellowship with the triune God in love for all conscious creation. The trust in God which causes one to leave off praying is not a trust which truly honors God. We may justly beware of a trust in God which makes us think that we are above the need of prayer.

The other objection to prayer comes in the name of law from popular science. We are told that this is a universe of uniform and necessary law; and hence prayer avails nothing. God governs the universe by uniform and immutable law; let us affirm this and believe this. Law is uniform, and no sane man thinks of changing law. But under this term "law" there lurks a subtle and dangerous fallacy. What do we mean by law? Law is simply the method which God adopts in the government of the universe. He is not a God of chance and change, but of order and uniformity. He is the All-orderly, the All-methodical. But law is not a power but a method. Man is under law, body, mind and spirit. But this does not mean that some power not himself determines every volition and thought. Man is under law, but law postulates human intelligence and volition in order that man may receive its benefit. Suppose we grant for a moment that all human actions are predetermined. Then we may claim that the act of prayer is predetermined also, and is a necessary link in the chain of causation. The reign of law in other departments of life does not mean that man is to do nothing to get a living; rather it postulates the conditions on which the man may live and grow. No one makes the reign of law a reason for doing nothing and making no effort to get a living. Effort is God's method of conferring benefits upon man. Prayer is as much a part of his method of blessing man as the falling rain, the growing seed, the ripening grain. What personal effort is in the realm of seed planting and fruit gathering, prayer may be in the sphere of spiritual planting and harvesting. Prayer does not seek to change God's will or God's order; rather it honors his order and lifts us up into correspondence with his will. We are told in the name of a mistaken trust and a false science that whatever good God ordains will come round to us in his own good time. But in other spheres of life we do not so act. Good does not come round to the man who does nothing but wait and frets not himself. Success in any sphere of life comes round not by external law or patient trust, but only through personal effort and co-operation. Prayer is as necessary as any other exercise or effort of man. We do not of course fully know how our prayers are the means of bringing about spiritual results in others. But since God does not work without means our prayers are necessary. "Prayer is as welcome to God as it is indispensable to men. For God does not work without means. He does not thrust reforms upon the world before the world is ready to receive them. The desires and petitions of individual hearts and united congregations are the signs by which the Spirit recognizes the fulness of time for spiritual and social advance" (Hyde: "Outlines of Social Theology," p. 131). In some way, we know not how, prayer brings God into the field, personally, actively, urgently manifesting himself. Prayer avails with God; it comes into his ear; it moves his heart; it calls forth his help. No one can read the Scriptures without seeing this; no one can believe in God without believing this. Men's prayers are far more to God than they dare hope; they accomplish far more than men ever know. It may be that men's prayers to God do more toward the blessing and saving of the world than all their words to men.

> "More things are wrought by prayer
> Than this world dreams of. Wherefore, let thy voice
> Rise like a fountain for me night and day.
> For what are men better than sheep or goats
> That nourish a blind life within the brain,
> If, knowing God, they lift not hands of prayer
> Both for themselves and those who call them friend?

For so the whole round earth is every way
Bound by gold chains about the feet of God."
—TENNYSON: *The Passing of Arthur.*

II. THE THREE ELEMENTS OF PRAYER.

1. The element of worship. We may say that two elements enter into worship: thanksgiving and adoration. God is the great giver of the universe. Whatever man possesses is God's gift. A large part of prayer is just recognition of God's gifts and blessings. Thankfulness is one of the foundation principles of the right life. The fact is we keep the consciousness of God clear in our minds and hearts only by the grateful recognition of his goodness. Paul's words referring to the heathen are significant; these people knew God, but they glorified him not as God, neither were thankful. And soon they lost God out of their consciousness. The man who truly knows God, and truly knows how to pray, will often find that his prayers are nothing more than the outgoings of a deeply grateful heart. It is surprising how large an element thanksgiving plays in the prayers of the Psalmist. How often men are exhorted to come before him with thanksgivings and to show themselves grateful to his name. "Bless the Lord, O my soul, and forget not all his benefits," is a familiar refrain.

Along with this there is also adoration of God. Very suggestive is the order of petitions in that prayer which teaches how to pray. When we pray we are to say: "Our Father who art in heaven, hallowed be thy name." To have right thoughts of God is all important. Prayer is the soul of man thinking its deepest thoughts in the presence of the heavenly Father. In prayer the soul of man is earnestly fixed upon God. No chapter in all the history of mankind is more tragic than that which shows how deplorably men have failed to appreciate the character of God. Every age, every nation has more or less disgraced itself and dishallowed God's name by setting up unworthy views of him. Too often men have made gods after their own image, in their own likeness. Prayer is the deepest and truest part of man searching after the deepest and truest knowledge of God.

2. The element of confession also holds a prominent place in prayer. The moment a soul begins to think rightly of God and to aspire after him, it becomes conscious of its own unfitness and unworthiness. Like a shock there comes to it a sense of its own sinfulness and shortcoming. No man can truly know God without knowing himself also. Job once had a kind of knowledge of God, half conviction, half hearsay. But through a bitter experience he is led into a deeper knowledge of the Eternal. Now he cries: "I have heard of thee by the hearing of the ear: but now mine eye seeth thee, wherefore I abhor myself, and repent in dust and ashes." Here comes out the point in the striking parable of the Master on prayer. The Pharisee is not really thanking God or aspiring

after God. He says in words: "God, I thank thee that I am not as other men," but for every thought he gives to God he gives ten to himself. He is thinking far more of what he has become than of what God has done. His prayer shows no deep heart-hunger for God; so it shows no deep consciousness of need, and it is destitute of confession and contrition. The publican has forgotten all about himself in thinking of the God above him. He is aspiring after God, trying to keep step with the eternal Father. And only one word is logical and fitting: God be merciful to me, a sinner.

The greatest sin of all, it has been said, is to be conscious of no sin. No man has learned to pray till there wells up in him a great sense of unworthiness before God. So he brings every part of his life, every plan, every effort, every ambition, and spreads them out before God for his testing and approval or rejection. Let a man think for a moment of the mixed motives with which he does his best work; let him think of the many things he does that are defective and wrong, and he will be filled exceedingly with confusion of face. Often he will run into the Inner Room where in secret he may pour out his story of failure and sin into the ear of the Father who heareth with such infinite patience and such infinite helpfulness.

3. The third element is communion. Prayer is the outgoing of the soul after God. All confidences enter into this exercise; and whatever con-

cerns the soul may go into the prayer to God. The true child consults his Father about everything. He has no wish, no plan that he cannot take to the Father for approval or for censure. The child takes the cares of the day and talks them over with the Father; he breathes out his wishes and longings into the ear that is ever ready to hear.

This element is too much overlooked in prayer. Many persons think of prayer as petition alone. So they seldom go to God unless they have some special favor to ask at his hands. The man who prays in this way does not know how to pray at all; he does not know the first elements of prayer. Prayer, real prayer is the longing of the soul after God and a ready acceptance of his will. The soul may go to God with some special petition, but as it communes with the Father, it begins to enter into God's purposes and plans for the world. Before the prayer is finished, the soul has made its confession of sin, its consecration to God's will and work, and is ready to ask what it can do toward the fulfillment of the thing desired. In every true petition there is somewhere wrapped up a vow to do God's will. One day the Master bade his disciples look over the crowd of fainting, scattered, shepherdless people. Then he charged them to pray the Lord of the harvest that he would send forth laborers into the harvest. Very significant, is the record that follows. And he called unto him his twelve disciples, and sent them out to heal every sickness and every infirmity. The man who prays, Father, thy kingdom come, waits upon God till he knows what he can do to help on the coming of that kingdom. A prayer that does not contain a vow is the most empty thing in the world. The Christian offers his prayer in the name of Christ: and the "name" signifies the character and will of Christ. That is, the man who prays in the name of Christ, enters into the spirit of Christ's life; he pledges himself to do whatever the Father wills. To pray in the name of Christ thus signifies to pray in the spirit of Christ, to seek the things which Christ seeks, to turn the soul over to the Father's will to be used as he directs.

Communion is the best part of prayer. We read that Jesus spent whole nights in prayer to God. We can hardly suppose that he spent all the hours in making requests of the Father. Rather we must suppose that he spent the precious hours in communion. Men misunderstood, hated him, rejected him; the burden of human woe pressed heavily upon his heart. He must get away from men that he may spend much time in communion with his Father. It was in prayer, we may believe, that he received the strength which enabled him to bear the sorrows and burdens of men. It was in prayer that he received the full consciousness of his oneness with the Father. And it was in prayer that he became transfigured with the glory of the eternal throne. "As he prayed, the fashion of his countenance was altered." The weakness and weariness vanish, and the power and glory of God fill his whole body with light. Moses, when he came down from the mount after forty days communion with God, came down with shining face. "Think of Buddha," says the Buddhist, "and you become like Buddha. If you pray to Buddha and do not become like Buddha, the mouth prays and not the heart." "But we all, with unveiled face, reflecting as a mirror the glory of the Lord, are transformed into the same image from glory unto glory, even as from the Lord the Spirit."

III. THE THREE KINDS OF PRAYER.

George Matheson in a suggestive chapter on "The Moral Place of Prayer," has analyzed prayers into three classes. Adopting his classification we name these: the prayer that is unheard; the prayer that is merely natural; and the prayer that is moral and Christian.

1. The prayer that is unheard is a more common prayer than many suppose. Many passages of Scripture might be quoted in illustration of this kind of prayer. "He that turneth away his ear from hearing the law, even his prayer shall be abomination" (Prov. xxviii. 9). Akin to this is the prayer of the man whose hands are full of guilt and whose heart is full of greed. "And when ye come to appear before me, who hath required this at your hand, to trample my courts? Bring no

more vain oblations: incense is an abomination unto me... And when ye spread forth your hands I will hide mine eyes from you; yea, when ye make many prayers I will not hear; your hands are full of blood" (Isaiah i. : 13, 15). No man can offer a right and acceptable prayer to God, unless he is trying to know God's will. For example: a godless man, whose life is one long disobedience, in some hour of danger cries unto God for help. He prays that God may spare the life of his child or may grant him some favor. Unless he comes saying, Oh, God, thy will be done in me and by me, Oh, God show me thy will and I will do it, his prayer is a hollow mockery, an abomination unto God. The first prayer that such a man can offer is a prayer for pardon and a pledge to obey. Shakespeare has expressed this truth in most striking words. The king has been conscience stricken by the scene enacted before him by Hamlet's trained players. He is alone now and tries to pray,—

> " O my offence is rank, it smells to heaven;
> It hath the primal eldest curse upon it,
> A brother's murder. Pray can I not;
> Though inclination be as sharp as will,
> My stronger guilt defeats my strong intent;
> And, like a man to double business bound,
> I stand in pause where I shall first begin,
> And both neglect. What if this cursed hand
> Were thicker than itself with brother's blood,
> Is there not rain enough in the sweet heavens

> To wash it white as snow? Whereto serves mercy
> But to confront the visage of offence?
> And what's in prayer but this twofold force,
> To be forestalled ere we come to fall,
> Or pardon'd being down? Then I'll look up;
> My fault is past. But, O, what form of prayer
> Can serve my turn? '*Forgive me my foul murder?*'
> That cannot be: since I am still possess'd
> Of those effects for which I did the murder,
> My crown, mine own ambition, and my queen.
> May one be pardon'd and retain the offence?
> . . . What then? What rests?
> Try what repentance can? what can it not?
> Yet what can it, when one cannot repent?
> O wretched state! O bosom black as death!
> O limèd soul, that, struggling to be free,
> Art more engaged! Help, angels! Make assay!
> Bow, stubborn knees: and heart, with strings of steel,
> Be soft as sinews of the new born babe!
> All may be well.
> (*Rising*) My words fly up, my thoughts remain below,
> Words without thoughts never to heaven go."
> *Hamlet*, Act III, Sc. 3.

The man who cherishes a known sin cannot offer an acceptable prayer to God. His only prayer that will be heard is a cry for pardon, a prayer that God will take away the sin, root and branch, out of his life. Till he does this, any other prayer is an abomination in the sight of God.

> " Who shall ascend into the hill of the Lord?
> And who shall stand in his holy place?

> He that hath clean hands, and a pure heart;
> Who hath not lifted up his soul unto vanity,
> And hath not sworn deceitfully.
> He shall receive a blessing from the Lord,
> And righteousness from the God of his salvation."
> *Psalm* 24 : 35.

From beginning to end of Scripture this is the constant refrain; for God to hear and bless, hands must be clean of greed and fraud, and the heart must be pure from covetousness and passion. This does not mean that no one can pray whose life is defective, but it does mean that no one can pray so long as he is willing to allow any defect to remain in his life.

Akin to this is the purely selfish prayer. "Ye ask, and receive not, because ye ask amiss, that ye may spend it in your pleasures" (James 4 : 3). The man's prayer may come from a perfectly sincere heart; and yet it is unheard because it is wrong. It is selfish through and through. His only thought of God is of one who can be used to further the selfish plans of men. More than we suppose of human prayers are unanswered, because they are little else than thinly disguised selfishness. So long as God can be persuaded to further his interests the man is homageful and reverent. A man is aspiring after some office in the state; and he promises God that, if elected, he will turn over a new leaf and become a church-member. Such a prayer as that is an abomination in the sight of God. Or, a man who desires to be rich promises

God that, if he becomes rich, he will do good with his money, and will give largely to the cause of missions. But God is not mocked. The attempt to cheat and hoodwink God in this way, by using him as a means for the gratification of our private whims and ambitions, is most futile. It requires no words to show that such prayers cannot be acceptable to the God of truth.

Another form of this unheard prayer is the purely personal prayer. What a man wishes for himself is to be the measure of his wish for all mankind. No man who has rightly known the God and Father of our Lord Jesus Christ can offer a purely personal prayer. He will make his own interest and wish subordinate to the will of God and the interests of his fellows. George Matheson supposes the case of two armies on the eve of battle holding religious services, and each army petitioning God for success on the morrow, which means the extermination of its antagonist. "We have no hesitation in saying that the New Testament would not indorse such a form of prayer. The most it would authorize in such circumstances would be the petition: "Thy kingdom come"— let that cause triumph, whose triumph would least disturb the balance of the empire of the King of kings" (Landmarks of the New Testament Morality, p. 122). How many prayers never get beyond the charmed circle of a man's own interests?" Some one has put this thought into the following selfish man's prayer,—

"God bless me and my wife,
My son John and his wife,
Us four and no more,
For Christ's sake. Amen."

In that prayer which teaches to pray, we are bidden to say :

"*Our* Father, who art in heaven, forgive *us*, lead *us*, deliver *us*."

In such a world as this, where men suffer, and sin, and starve, a purely personal prayer is an unacceptable, an unheard prayer.

2. Next above this in the scale, we have the natural prayer, the prayer of the man who has no true knowledge of the will and character of God, the Gentile prayer, as Christ called it. Against this kind of prayer we are cautioned by the Master : " Be not anxious for your life, what ye shall eat, or what ye shall drink, nor yet for your body what ye shall put on—For after all these things do the Gentiles seek ; for your heavenly Father knoweth that ye have need of all these things." This kind of prayer is not described as immoral, but it is Gentile in its spirit, in that it rises no higher than the level of pagan thought. Many times in his teaching Jesus drew contrasts between the morality of the Gentiles and the righteousness of the kingdom. He does not condemn their ideas and moralities as immoral or illegitimate, but only shows how far short they come of the saintly and the Christian standard. The Gentile mind takes

anxious thought for the things of time and sense; food and raiment, treasure and ease bulk large in its interest. After all these things do the Gentiles seek; but the Christian is to live on a higher plane. Notice that Jesus does not forbid men asking for these other things of food and raiment; he only says that the prayer that never rises above these things is Gentile and not Christian. The man who is living for the present world, who is concerned chiefly for the body and its wants, who never rises in prayer above the natural and the temporal, has not yet entered into the glory of the kingdom of God. This does not mean that we are never to take to God our temporal and everyday interests; concerning everything we are to consult him. But much depends upon the kind of thought we give to these things; much depends upon the motive in the prayer. The difference, as Matheson so well shows, lies in the motive and the thought, whether the things are sought as means or as ends. We have the warrant of Scripture in praying for blessings upon men, blessings of fruitful seasons and temporal prosperity. But ours is a Gentile prayer, if it rises no higher than these material things. These things have value, in so far as they minister to the life of the soul. Much working and planning and praying is Gentile and not Christian, for the simple reason that it never gets above the level of the material and the earthly. The man lives in the kingdom of this world; he does not see that the life is more than the meat, and the man is more than the raiment. He does not see that a man's life consisteth not in the abundance of the things which he possesseth. Christ's own order in his model prayer is given for our guidance. The Father's name, the Father's kingdom, the Father's will come first; then, as means to these ends, we pray for daily bread, for deliverance from evil, and for all other things. This is the determining question: Do we regard the Father's kingdom as a means to our daily bread; or do we regard our daily bread as a means to the Father's kingdom? "After such things do the Gentiles seek; and your Father knoweth that ye have need of these things. But seek ye first the kingdom of God and his righteousness, and all these things shall be added unto you." Matt. 6 : 32, 33.

3. And this brings us to the highest kind of prayer, the fully Christian prayer. In this prayer the hallowing of God's name, the coming of God's kingdom, and the doing of God's will are supreme ends; and all other things are means toward these ends. What was said above applies here: God's greatest gift to men is himself. The Christian prayer is a prayer that men may know God rather than anything that he has to bestow. It is a prayer that we may make his name, his kingdom, his will higher than our own interests and pleasures and desires. The Christian has an interest in everything human; he seeks daily bread and proper clothing. But these things are all glorified

and transfigured by the kingdom of God of which they are a part. God's name, God's kingdom, God's will he sees are universal, loving, social. His seeking of bread is no longer a personal thing, but a participation in the universal hunger of the world. He sees that he is a member of the great body of humanity, and he makes its pains and wants his own burden and care. He seeks and prays now that all men may become partakers in the common bounties and blessings of God. Out of his deep sense of oneness with his fellows, in all their sorrows and joys, their woes and wants, he lifts his soul in prayer to the heavenly Father in their behalf.

> " He prayeth well, who loveth well
> Both man, and bird and beast.
>
> He prayeth best, who loveth best
> All things both great and small;
> For the dear God who loveth us,
> He made and loveth all."
>   COLERIDGE: *The Ancient Mariner.*

Thus prayer, true Christian prayer, is more than petition to God, it is more also than communion with God; it is rather participation in the life of God, it is the soul of man aspiring after God's will and the glory of his kingdom. This prayer has its human aspects and outlooks as well. It is more than petitioning God for men, more than an intercession in their behalf. Rather it is a participation in the life of man and an aspiration to bring the blessings of God's kingdom into the lives of all men, a longing to bring God and man together in a fellowship of life and love. Prayer, Christian prayer, seeks to lift man up to God, and to bring God near to man. The Christian enters into his closet, but his thought goes out to all mankind. He says there in the Inner Room : " Our Father : forgive us our debts, give us our daily bread, lead us not into temptation, but deliver us from evil."

And such prayers move in the realm of moral certainty because they possess moral value. Concerning all such prayers there can be no question but that they are heard and answered. Such prayers are truly offered in the name and spirit of the Lord Jesus ; such prayers are truly in accord with the will of God. Over against all such prayers there stands recorded the promise : " Whatsoever ye shall ask in my name, that will I do."

And in this conception of prayer we find the harmony of the two injunctions of Scripture : First, that of the Lord Jesus : " When ye pray, enter into your closet and shut the door." And the other word of the apostle Paul : " Pray without ceasing." The man who prays the Christian's prayer will desire to get away from the bustle and crowd of the street ; he will long to be alone with God for a season. In that closet the keynote of his life will be struck ; in that closet the attitude of his soul will be determined. Then he arises and goes out to make his life an aspiration, and to show this attitude of his soul by his endeavor. His life becomes a prayer, and his prayer determines his life.

CHAPTER V.

PAST THE DEAD POINTS.

He that is unrighteous, let him do unrighteousness yet more; and he that is filthy, let him be made filthy yet more; and he that is righteous, let him do righteousness yet more; and he that is holy, let him be made holy yet more.—*The Apocalypse, R. V. and Margin.*

In the conduct of life, habits count for more than maxims, because habit is a living maxim, become flesh and instinct. To reform one's maxims is nothing; it is but to change the title of the book. To learn new habits is everything, for it is to reach the substance of life. Life is but a tissue of habits.—HENRI-FREDERIC AMIEL.

There is peril in cutting loose from the habitual and the stated. Disposition needs training. Character is impulse that has been reined down into steady continuance.—CHARLES H. PARKHURST.

Sow an act, and you reap a habit; sow a habit, and you reap a character; sow a character, and you reap a destiny.—GEORGE DANA BOARDMAN.

INERTIA is the power that resists change. It may be called the conservative principle of the universe. It is the friend of order, stability, and permanence. Without it the order of the universe could not be maintained for an instant. Some one has given a fancy sketch of a world in which levity took the place of gravity. A sketch even more fanciful might be made of a world in which inertia had no place. Inertia is defined in the school-books as that property of matter by which it cannot of itself change its own state of motion or of rest. No particle of matter in the universe has power to move itself when at rest ; and no particle of matter has power to stop itself when in motion. There is thus an inherent and constant tendency in things to continue in their present state. It is said that a stone thrown into the air would continue in a straight line forever were it not for the resistance of the air and the attraction of the earth.

Inertia holds an honorable place in all human affairs. Because of this principle the steam-engine is possible. Without a fly-wheel the steam-engine would practically be impossible. The piston-rod, pushed by the power of the steam, moves out in its course and then comes to a dead stop. But while the rod is moving out in its course, it is storing up energy in the fly-wheel. When the piston-rod has reached its limit, it comes to the dead-point and is helpless. But the stored-up energy in the wheel now asserts itself and carries the rod past the dead-point. Thus regular motion is maintained and the engine becomes possible. Inertia can say to men : they reckon ill who leave me out.

This property of things that we call inertia, when read in terms of matter, we call habit when read in terms of life. Habit is to life what inertia is to matter. What we are, we tend to continue ; what we are not, it is not easy to become. And in this principle that men call habit we find the promise and potency of progress and growth. Habit stores up the effort and energy of the past, and carries life past its dead-points. It thus insures patient continuance in well-doing. Habit, like inertia, keeps the motion of life steady and unbroken, and distributes the man's power equally and regularly over the work to be done.

I. The Law of Habit.

Habit is three-fourths of life. Some one has called man a bundle of habits. Nine-tenths of all the things we think or say or do, we think or say or do, because we are in the habit of so doing. We could do very little in this world, were it not for this principle of habit. Habit conserves the effort of the past and makes it available in the present. The formation of right habits means a great saving of physical and mental energy and effort. Our life builds itself up out of the things we do from day to day. No act begins or ends with itself. Everything we do is built into the structure of life, and becomes at once an effect and a cause; we may say that every act is an effect that becomes a cause. A Spanish proverb says: "Every man is the child of his own deeds." And just as truly may we say: "Every man's deeds are the children of all his past." What we have done is a prophecy of what we will do. A simple illustration will make this truth plain.

A number of men determine to build a railroad through a certain country. They find many obstacles in the way: hills have to be leveled, valleys must be filled, grades must be determined, and curves calculated. By and by, however, the road is built and the rails are laid. Now every train passing through that country has its course all marked out for it. The engine has nothing to do but follow along lines long ago determined for it. To-day the train passes over a course determined for it fifty years ago. It is precisely so with man. In his early years he is making a course for himself, laying down certain lines of action, creating certain habits of thought and speech. As the years pass the man becomes very largely the mere copy of himself; he does very few original things; he continues to be just what he has been. And more than this, all things here below tend toward a permanence. For a number of years the brain of man is plastic, and is easily influenced by new conditions and shaped to new issues. But in the course of years the brain cells assume a more and more fixed structure; thus new modes of thought and activity become increasingly difficult. The water in running down a valley soon wears a channel for itself; and as the channel is worn the stream runs. A time comes when the man has determined a channel for his life; then just as the channel is made the life runs. The changing of old courses of life becomes difficult and the acquirement of new courses becomes more and more difficult. Our present is the resultant of our past, and our present is the determiner of our future. Our physical, mental and moral life tends to become fixed and unchangeable. New impressions may come to us, but they have little influence; new appeals may be made, but they become less and less potent. The man yields to that which falls in with his habitual modes of thought and action. The number of persons converted when above fifty years of age is significantly small, so small that we can say to the youth: it is now or never. Thus what men do in youth becomes an angel or a nemesis to bless or to plague them in the years to come. Life has no breaks; we shall be to-morrow just what we are to-day, only more so. The man who reaches fifty years of age shiftless, intemperate, prayerless, is almost certain to remain such to the end of the chapter. "Can the Ethiopian change his skin, or the leopard his spots? Then may those who are accustomed to do evil, learn to do well." Change is not impossible, else life would be a most hopeless and tragic affair. But any change that may come to life is simply a change in the direction of action. No change can ever bring to man a set of new habits ready made and perfect. Conversion, as men call it, puts in the warp on which life weaves a new fabric.

Habit is thus one of the great and fateful facts of human life. Habits are extremely useful or extremely hurtful, just according to the nature of the habit. This principle of habit makes progress both possible or impossible. The formation of good habits results in a saving of incalculable effort and pain. This power of habit enables us to do our daily work with the least expenditure of thought and effort. Suppose we had to learn how to speak every time we wanted to utter a word. Suppose we had to learn how to make the letters every time we wanted to write a sentence. Suppose we had to acquire the art of playing every time we sat down to the piano. To learn to do these things was not easy. But now that we have learned how to do them, they almost do themselves. We sit down to the desk with paper and pen, and think a word, and the word practically writes itself. Speaking, writing, walking, and a thousand other things are done almost automatically and mechanically. We think the thing, and lo, it is done without conscious effort. Dexterity in work, the power of speech, the mode of expressing one's self, all have to be acquired by infinite care and effort. When once they are acquired, they become a permanent possession, and thus man is enabled to give his attention to other things.

No one can overestimate the significance and value of habits. All man's actions tend to become fixed, automatic and unchangeable. A great many people suppose that they can cease to do ill, and learn to do well at any time, whenever they choose. One good resolution does not make a man holy, as one warm day does not make a spring. No man can "resolve" a bad habit out of his life and "resolve" a good habit in at a moment's notice. The law of inertia will not permit any such thing. It

is a good thing for man that it is so. If character
could be gained in a moment, it could be lost in a
moment. Easy come, easy go, is as true in morals
as in money. Whatever is worth having must be
worked for ; it is not gained by wishing. After
all, this should give man joy rather than pain.
The virtue that is easily won is as easily lost. The
man who is hard to move is hard to stop when
going. No power beneath the stars could stop
Saul the persecuter of the Christians ; and no
power beneath those same stars could stop Paul
the apostle. Paul is Saul with a new Master, a
new direction in life. Beginnings are always difficult, but as one goes on the power to continue
increases. After a time one can continue on without effort. There is a kind of momentum in life,
which carries one onward with accelerating speed
and force in whatever direction he is going. One's
smallest acts are big with destiny. Does this seem
to make life a fatal and inexorable thing ? Well,
there are tremendous and inevitable conditions that
hedge in the life of man. There is an apparent
fatalism about all this, but it is the fatalism of
character. There is a tremendous inveteracy in our
deeds. We have the power of determining what our
habits shall be, but when once these habits are
formed we must accept the result. The man who
chooses the left-hand road must not complain because he is not rewarded with right-hand goals.
The man who knowingly takes a steamer for Liverpool must not complain because he is not landed

at Hamburg. The man who puts out in the current that carries away from God and good, must not be surprised if soon or late he goes over the falls. This life of man's is no haphazard, chance thing. No; great and inevitable conditions shut him in on every side; his only safety consists in knowing these conditions, as his only blessedness consists in adjusting himself to the nature of things. Character is the sum total of one's habits; and character is destiny. "Heaven is character," said Confucius. Man is the maker of his destiny, because he is the maker of his habits.

II. The Place of Habit in Man's Life.

1. In man's physical life this law applies with great force. Every one remembers how difficult it was to learn to write. At the head of the page were the letters to be copied, but somehow the hand could not form the letters in imitation of the copy. But hour after hour we practised and toiled, till the hand acquired a certain skill and dexterity. Now the letters come of themselves as we think them. We stored up a vast amount of energy in the muscles and nerves of the hand, and now we form the letters without effort. What is true here is true in all parts of man's physical being. Wm. B. Carpenter speaks "from long and varied experience of the immense saving of exertion which arises from the formation of methodical habits of mental labor; which cause the ordinary routine to be performed with a far less amount of fatigue,

than would be required on a more desultory system" (Mental Physiology, p. 350). This same writer says that he has been led to regard military drill as an important part of education; not merely as promoting a healthy physical development, and as preparing every youth, if occasion should require, to serve in the ranks of national defenders, but even more for the moral value of the enforcement of strict order and discipline, and prompt obedience to the word of command. Wellington said that he won Waterloo on the playground at Eton. This is how Victor Hugo characterizes the two commanders who confronted one another at Waterloo. " On one side, precision, foresight, geometry, prudence, a retreat assured, reserves prepared, an obstinate coolness, imperturbable method, strategy profiting by the ground, tactics balancing battalions, carnage measured by a plumb-line, war regulated watch in hand, nothing left voluntarily to accident, old classic courage and absolute correctness. On the other side we have intuition, divination, military strangeness, superhuman instinct, a flashing glance; something that gazes like the eagle, and strikes like lightning, all the mysteries of a profound mind, association with destiny; the river, the plain, the forest and the hill summoned and to some extent compelled to obey, the despot going so far as to tyrannize over the battle-field; faith in a star blended with strategic science, heightening but troubling it. . . . True genius was conquered by calculation. On both sides somebody was expected; and it was the exact calculator who succeeded. Napoleon waited for Grouchy who did not come; Wellington waited for Blücher and he came" (*Les Miserables*).

A keen observer has said that he can stand at a street corner and tell the kind of work that nine out of ten persons are doing by the way they walk, swing their arms and move their fingers. Every man is binding himself in cords that cannot be broken. By choice or by necessity a man engages in certain kinds of work. The habitual activity reacts upon the mind and determines the habitual mode of thought. Herodotus tells of a tribe of Scythians who, during the absence of their masters, had taken possession of their property and homes. Several battles were fought and the slaves proved themselves good soldiers. Then one of the Scythians proposed another line of attack; he advised the masters to lay aside their bows and spears and to provide themselves with whips. The masters advanced against their old slaves cracking their whips, and the slaves astonished at this, forgot to fight, fled in confusion and were easily conquered. Old habit was stronger than new resolve.

2. The great difference between men is found here in this power of habit. We all know that men come into the world differently endowed mentally, but the difference in actual mental capacity is not so great as we sometimes suppose. Men differ most widely in their mental habits, in those habits which count so much in life. George Eliot defined

genius as an infinite capacity for taking pains. Buffon said it was patience. Sir Isaac Newton said that he differed from other men only in the power of patient thought. Sir Wm. Hamilton has declared that the difference between an ordinary mind and Newton's is this : the one was capable of a continuous attention, while the other soon dropped the thread of thought which he had begun to spin. Expert accountants say that the books of nine out of ten bankrupts are in a muddle; they have been kept without plan or method. Many people ignorantly suppose that the great artists and poets of the world have done their great work without effort and practice. No greater mistake can be made. The masterpieces of the world represent an amount of toil that is appalling to the ordinary man. The best talent in this world is the habit of careful, continuous, absorbing work.

Nothing can be more certain than that any sequence of mental action which has been frequently repeated tends to perpetuate itself without any consciously formed purpose. The same thoughts tend to recur whenever the same circumstances are present. The number of persons who have complete control of their habits of thought is exceedingly small. We are all too much at the mercy of chance incidents and accidents. We do not *think ;* we only allow impressions to run riot in our minds. If one wants to know how little control he has over his own thought, let him try a simple experiment. Let him repeat the Lord's Prayer without thinking of anything else, except the words he is saying. Probably not one person in ten thousand can do this. The man who has formed the habit of continuous, absorbing, attentive work is the man, all other things being equal, who has all the world before him.

3. What is true in man's physical and mental life is not less true in his moral. Habit counts for as much here as in any other part of life. In our moral life, to-day is the child of yesterday. What we are to-day we shall be to-morrow, only a little more so. Character knows no breaks. Most people are living in the delusion that one of these days they will drop off their bad habits and put on new habits. Sad delusion, fatal mistake! Men appreciate the wrongfulness of the things they do from hour to hour, but too few take into account the weight of the habit. Agassiz, it is said, once wanted to examine the interior of an Alpine glacier, and was lowered by two men into a deep chasm. He gave the signal to be drawn up, but the men who had lowered him found themselves unable to raise him out of the pit. They had calculated the weight of his body and the weight of the basket, but had forgotten the weight of the rope that descended with him. The explorer was obliged to remain in the pit till help could be summoned. The weight of the rope that goes down with one into the pit of habit is a fact in this universe, and the wise man takes it into his reckoning.

Say what men will about total depravity, man

has no natural talent for doing right. Righteousness is a kind of art that must be acquired, like any other art. A recent writer has called his book: "Conduct as a Fine Art." The title is well chosen and illustrates a great truth. Nine-tenths of the vicious desires that tempt men and degrade society would shrink into comparative insignificance before the advance of careful self-discipline, self-control, and habitual attention. It is by the watchful and continuous exercise of these qualities that purity of heart, control of imagination, energy of will are secured, and built up into chastity, temperance and force. "To him that hath shall be given, and from him that hath not shall be taken away even that which he seemeth to have." To him who loves truth more truth shall be given. The tendency of good is toward more good, as the tendency of evil is toward more evil. Every man thus becomes his own angel or his own nemesis. Ephraim made altars to sin; and altars became to him a temptation to more sin. What a man is, he continues to be; what he is not it is not easy to become. The man who is earnest, godly, prayerful to-day, tends to become more earnest, more godly, more prayerful to-morrow.

No man's virtue can be called safe and strong till it has become habitual. The world is full of men who have good impulses in plenty. Browning says that the worst man knows better than the best man does. However that may be, any man may know, if he will follow on to know. But good impulses alone are the most vain and useless things in the world. "Hell is paved with good intentions," not with good habits. To say that a man has good impulses is often the worst thing that can be said of him. Many a man who has plenty of good impulses is slowly, surely, inevitably drifting down toward the bottomless pit. Habit ensures permanence in good courses; it also ensures permanence in evil courses. Habit carries a man heavenward or hellward with equal force and irresistibleness. "He that is unrighteous, let him do unrighteousness yet more; and he that is filthy, let him be made filthy yet more; and he that is righteous, let him do righteousness yet more; and he that is holy, let him be made holy yet more" (Rev. 22 : 11, R. V. and margin). A systematic organization of the habits of life is the necessary means toward all progress in right character. The wing of right and habitual resolution, which is so mighty to lift us nearer God, can only be formed by patient continuance in right doing.

III. THE RIGHT HABITS WHICH GO INTO THE MAKING OF RIGHT CHARACTER. Without attempting to go into detail it may be worth while to notice a few of those habits which are so all-important in the formation and maintenance of right life. We mention three or four activities of the progressively right life which it is not safe to leave unregulated. It is all very well to speak of "spontaneous goodness," but spontaneous goodness that amounts to much is the overflow of a regulated soul.

The man whose piety is left to chance impulses will have a most irregular and fluctuating piety. Unless he has acquired considerable momentum, he will stick at the dead-points. I remember, as a boy, when riding with my father, seeing him whip up the horses before he came to a bad bit of road. The momentum usually carried us through all right. One must learn to do good by rule and method, before he will be able to do good by impulse and desire. Here, as in other lines, the law is our schoolmaster to bring us unto Christ.

1. Take first the matter of prayer. "Evening, and morning, and at noon, will I pray." That was what we may call systematic piety, methodical goodness, clockwork religion. Some one at once objects to this, and says that this fosters formalism and hollowness. Perhaps it does; but it also promotes true piety and prayerfulness. The man who has formed the habit of prayer at certain times and places, finds that time and place have much to do with the mood of prayer. The very fact that one is in the place of prayer, on his knees, will do much to promote the prayerful spirit. At any rate, chance impulses cannot be relied on in this matter of prayer. Man's needs are daily, hourly needs; his consciousness of those needs is by no means daily or hourly. The man who does not pray, except when he feels just like

it, will not pray very much. The prayerful spirit comes from the prayerful habit. A man's prayer in the morning may have been somewhat cold and formal, but he is far more likely to have a thought of God through the hours of toil, because of this, than if he had neglected prayer because he was not in the mood for it. The habit of prayer will thus carry one over those points in life when the spirit flags and impulse is wanting. There are times in almost every life, dead-points, when faith seems all gone, impulse is weak, the spiritual life seems to have waned, and the power to resolve is lacking. This is the turning-point in life, the test of character. Happy is he whose life has acquired sufficient momentum to carry the man over these dead-points.

Of Daniel in Babylon, we read that three times a day he made his prayers unto God. Three times a day he was to be found in the same place, at the same window, with his face turned in a certain direction. Some one makes light of this, and says that it is mere clockwork religion, arithmetical piety, methodical goodness. Perhaps so ; but it is well to remember that Daniel was a perfectly safe man in any emergency. It was possible to forecast the spiritual latitude and longitude of that man at any hour of the day or night. And that is probably a hundred times as much as can be said of the man who is prayerful by impulse and feeling.

2. A habit of Bible study is also most valuable. If

the Bible is what men believe it to be, the revelation of the person, character, and will of the eternal God, if it is the record which God gave of his Son, if the truths therein defined are able to make men wise unto salvation, surely men should become familiar with this book. The common objection is made that men have not time for full, elaborate, or even extensive study of the Scriptures. Life is to the average man a hard and engrossing struggle for existence, and not much time can be given in any day to study. But probably not one person in ten thousand is so driven as to make systematic and regular Bible study impossible. Fifteen minutes a day spent in careful and thoughtful study of the Bible will, in the course of a few years, give one a very satisfactory idea of the great teachings, persons, events, lessons, of the Scripture record. By all means let this study be regular and systematic. Desultory Bible reading, like everything else desultory, is almost barren of results. He is the healthy man whose appetite is regular and who is always hungry at certain times. Regularity in eating is at once a sign of health and a cause of health. However it may be with man's body, his soul needs its food at regular hours and in daily portions. Joshua is charged to meditate upon the book of the law day and night, and is assured that then he shall make his way prosperous, and then he shall have good success. Bible study, like prayer, cannot be left to chance impulse and feeling. For with almost every one, there are times when impulse is wanting; the life comes to one of its dead-points. This is the time of all others when the man most needs the Bible. The days in which we feel least like prayer and Bible study, are the very days in which we most need them. He who has formed the habit of prayer and Bible study has acquired sufficient momentum of soul to carry him past these seasons without failure or spiritual decline. Habit thus conserves one's best impulses and makes them efficient in one's weakest hours. Habit, like the fly-wheel on the engine, keeps the motion of life steady and unbroken, and distributes the force of man's better moods equally over the whole of life.

3. What is true of prayer and Bible study is true, none the less of all forms of Christian service. To be a disciple of Christ means to engage in some kind of work for others. It is for each disciple to know his own aptitudes and to follow the leadings of the Spirit. No rule can be laid down as to the kind and amount of such work that shall be done. But whatever is done, let it be done by system. If one determines to do personal work, let him form the habit of daily exercise. The presence of the habit of doing good will make one watchful of opportunities. Mrs. Browning has said: "Most people are kind, if they only think of it." The habit makes one think of it. What a world this would soon become if it had a few more persons with the well-formed habit of doing good! In work of any kind faithfully and regularly done, there comes

a fine training for body, mind, and spirit. One thing is certain: the man who does good only when the impulse is strong will do good very irregularly. There is nothing in the world more unreliable than chance impulse, nothing more evanescent, nothing more irregular. The man who desires to make and maintain a fine Christian character will make his best moments the standard for his worst. He will form some high and worthy purpose in life, and will then resolutely set to work to form habits in fulfillment of that purpose. In this way the best impulses, the highest resolves, the choicest aspirations are conserved, and their power is distributed evenly and equally over the whole of life.

4. This truth is capable of almost indefinite expansion and application. Of all the habits that are of value to man, none can be of greater service than the reading habit in general. Literature is one of the important facts of modern life. We are the people upon whom the ends of the ages are come. The printing-press has made accessible to the lowliest, the best that has been thought and said in this world. The newspaper is omnipresent, and everybody reads it. There is little difficulty in persuading people to read: whether they read harmfully or helpfully is quite another question. Many persons read nothing but the newspapers, on the plea that they have no time for more substantial and regular reading. But this plea of "No time," is in nearly every case a transparent apology for indifference, or shiftlessness, or irregularity.

How strange, how tragic, that so many are content to spend all their spare time dozing over a newspaper, when the eternal books of the world are unknown to them! But here, as elsewhere, much depends upon the habit one has formed. The reading habit, like all others, is capable of indefinite cultivation. A taste for the great books, in some cases, may have to be acquired; the books best worth reading are not always the easiest reading. They demand, as they merit, careful and painstaking thought and attention. But this habit can easily be acquired, and when acquired it becomes a source of the keenest delight, a never-failing spring of helpfulness, a continual safeguard against evil. Give a boy a taste for good books, form in him the reading habit, and you need not have fears for that boy's future. Well might Fénelon say: "If the crowns of all the kingdoms of the empire were laid at my feet in exchange for my books and my love of reading, I would spurn them all."

The pressure of modern life makes extensive reading for the majority of persons impossible. But this is all the more reason why the fragments of time should be well used and richly treasured. This time is almost sure to be wasted, unless it is safeguarded and directed by system. It has been said that the whole world of mankind thinks itself busy, when it is wasting an untold amount of time. Perhaps not one person in a hundred has any idea of the amount of time he wastes every day. What is more, he cannot know, till he has resolutely set to work to employ usefully every moment. The habit of being usefully employed in reading is one of the best safeguards against wasting time in idle gossip, in dissipating newspaper-scanning, or in useless dreaming. An inch of time every day directed by system and earnestly hoarded will accomplish wonders. Sir John Lubbock used that inch of time out of banking hours, and became an authority on prehistoric studies. John Stuart Mill wrote his greatest book while closely engaged in the India Office. Elihu Burritt, the blacksmith, used his inch of time, and became one of the foremost linguists of his age. As a rule it will appear that the great books of the world have been written by busy men, by men who have toiled while others slept and have saved the moments which others wasted. The habit of regular methodical work will accomplish wonders here below. It is not so much lack of time that hinders men, as lack of method, lack of habit, lack of purpose. The man who is determined to excel must cease saying that he has no time for prayer, no time for Bible study, no time for God's work, no time for reading, no time for anything. Men prate over their busy lives, and then coddle themselves with the thought that they have no time. "Where there's a will, there's a way." The habits that are required for the efficient prosecution of any work are within the possibility of all; they are application, attention, accuracy, method, punctuality, thoughtfulness, regularity. The man who has formed these habits has all the world open before him; all the possibilities of the noblest living and achieving are his. Some may sneer at these things as trifles, unworthy of notice and cultivation. But as the highest mountain is made up of grains of sand; so the greatest life is made up of trifles. As the cents make the dollars, and the seconds make the hours; so the aggregation of things insignificant makes up human character. The regular repetition of little things makes character; and character makes life and destiny. The whole philosophy of life may be summed up in a sentence: Begin right, then keep on going.

CHAPTER VI.

THE LESS HONORED VIRTUES.

And having done all to stand. Stand therefore.—The Apostle Paul.

> Drop thy still dews of quietness,
>   Till all our strivings cease;
> Take from our souls the strain and stress;
>   And let our ordered lives confess
>   The beauty of thy peace.
>
> Breathe through the heats of our desire
>   Thy coolness and thy balm;
> Let sense be dumb, let flesh retire;
>   Speak through the earthquake, wind and fire,
>   O still, small voice of calm.
>   —J. G. Whittier: *The Brewing of Soma.*

We need resolutely and with pious obstinacy to set this temper before us, for it is not natural to our hearts. Even the best of us, in the excitement of our work, forget to think of anything except of making our mark, or of getting the better of what we are at work upon. When work grows hard, the combative instincts waken within us, till we look upon the characters God has given us to mould as enemies to be fought. We must ever remember that we are not warriors but artists,—artists after the fashion of Jesus Christ, who came not to condemn life because it was imperfect, but to build life up to the image of God. Creation is the certificate that no moral effort is a forlorn hope.—George Adam Smith: *Isaiah.*

Man, it has been observed, is a creature of moods and tenses. But he is also a creature of voice as well. He is a man of limited experience whose life can be conjugated in one mood or tense;

and he is a man of no less limited character whose qualities can be comprehended in one voice. Henry Martyn has said that life is summed up in three things: "to believe, to suffer, to love." The qualities which go to the making of right character are many and various. The world has made much of the active virtues of life; it has admired the forceful, the impetuous, the daring, the self-confident. Jesus Christ the Master in Virtue, makes much of what may be called the passive virtues. He commends and blesses the graces of humility, contentment, patience, and forgiveness. Christianity shows its pre-eminence, its finality, in the balance it maintains in life in making excellence of character consist in the harmonious combination of many forms of virtue. Harmony in music is the happy blending of many tones and not the monotonous repetition of one note. The pure white light, spectrum analysis shows, is the harmonious combination of the various prismatic colors.

The ideal of the world is very different from the ideal of Christ. The world inclines to honor the more conspicuous and forceful graces of life; it notices the great flaring chrysanthemum sooner than the humble violet hiding in the grass and only betraying its presence by its quiet fragrance. It is a fine and Christly thing to wage a good warfare when the battle is on; but it is no less a fine and Christly thing to stand on guard and wait for the daylight. Since we are concerned with the whole round of Christian character, it is fitting that we should consider the Citizen when called upon to endure and suffer and be patient. They serve the Lord who fight dragons, withstand wrong, and do exploits. But

"They also serve who only stand and wait."

I. THE PLACE WHICH THE PASSIVE VIRTUES HOLD IN THE CHRISTIAN VIEW OF LIFE. A great philosopher has said that we need a revised philosophy of life. However that may be, many of the opinions and sentiments that are current among men greatly need revising and Christianizing. On no question does opinion need revising more urgently, than on this question of what is great and heroic in life. Different ages and different peoples have cherished different opinions of what constitutes greatness. Among the Greeks he was the great man who possessed beauty of body and strength of limb, who could handle the sword and spear skillfully and never turned back to the foe. Among the Romans the ideal hero was the military leader, who had braved the hardships of war, crushed his enemies, and conquered new territory for Rome. Our Saxon ancestors had their own ideas and ideals of virtue and greatness. In their opinion the chief glory of man consisted in warlike achievements on the field of battle. An ancient song declares: "He who has never been wounded lives a weary life." Among them it was counted a reproach to reach old age and die of some disease.

The way to heaven lay through devastated towns and across the bodies of fierce enemies. They believed that the soul of the warrior who fell on the battle-field passed at once to the paradise of Odin, where he was blessed in being permitted to drink delightful meads from the skulls of his enemies. Some of the blood of those old Saxons flows in our veins, and though centuries have passed, and we have wandered far from the old home, we have not cast off the ancestral ideals, and our blood has not yet become wholly cooled to more temperate views. Among all races and in all ages the man of great physical strength and courage has been proclaimed chief and king. To-day the warlike, the strong, the forceful, the dashing, the successful, receive a large share of public praise and admiration. We build monuments to the great military leader; we weave chaplets and lay them upon the graves of the brave soldiers; we bow in respect before the man who by force and skill has won his way to wealth and position.

Not for a moment can we make less of these more heroic, more active, more forceful virtues. Without the moral energy which lies at the root of these virtues, the tenderest attachments of life and the most precious graces of the spirit degenerate more or less into weaknesses and immoralities. Still, in any right view of character, we must notice those complemental virtues which belong to the more inward and passive side of life. Right here Christianity makes issue with the whole world on the question of what constitutes human greatness and perfection. To do and dare is with the world a sign of greatness and courage; to bear and suffer is the mark of Christian worth. The doctrine of the cross is the proclamation of a new law of life and a new kind of glory. To Paganism, the most ignoble service in life was burden-bearing and suffering; to Christianity, the service of suffering and burden-bearing is of all others the noblest and divinest. Over-emphasis is always wrong. It is possible to cultivate one set of virtues at the expense of another, and thus the character becomes one-sided and imperfect. Christianity declares its pre-eminence, its sanity, in the balance it maintains among the virtues. It teaches us to see that these two forms of virtue are the complement the one of the other. A man all meekness, and patience, and forgiveness is a poor specimen of Christian virtue. On the other hand, a man all energy and force and enthusiasm lacks some of the necessary graces of Christian character. Bearing and suffering are as much a part of life as doing and daring.

It is worthy of note that the Lord Jesus gives great emphasis to these virtues in his life and teaching. The Sermon on the Mount, which in fine phrase has been called, "The Magna Charta of the Kingdom of God," opens with a series of beatitudes on character. The order of these beatitudes is worthy of notice; and, as we proceed, we shall see how widely the words of the Master differ from the words of other teachers. We shall see how squarely they cut across the ideas and opinions of the world. Popular opinion estimates men by what they have; Jesus pronounces men blessed for what they are. Jesus is not talking at random when he utters these beatitudes. These eight beatitudes describe not so much eight separate classes of men, as one man in whom are found eight characteristic virtues of the kingdom. They picture a Christly development of life from blessedness to blessedness, from its first beginning in poverty of spirit, to its perfected righteousness with God. The Christian disciple must go down into the Valley of Humility, before he can stand upon the heights of the Delectable Mountains owned and glorified as the Son of God. Blessed are the poor in spirit; blessed are they that mourn; blessed are the meek. Before Christ finishes the sermon we shall see this poor, mourning, meek man, filled with righteousness, given a vision of God, and manifested among men as the son of the Highest. The man who is poor, sorrowful, and meek to the very core is all emptied of self. He has gone down into the Valley of Humility, and patience and penitence have had their perfect work. Out of his conscious nothingness the man turns and hungers and thirsts after the righteousness of God. And three elements of this righteousness are named. Blessed are the merciful; blessed are the pure in heart; blessed are the peacemakers. Then in a closing beatitude the Master illustrates the relation of his disciple to the external world. The disciple who will follow the Master whithersoever he goeth, will suffer persecution; he will be misunderstood and maligned; in the world the disciple shall find no paradise but only persecution. "Blessed are ye when men shall revile you and persecute you, and shall say all manner of evil against you falsely, for my sake. Rejoice, and be exceeding glad: for great is your reward in heaven: for so persecuted they the prophets which were before you." All through the sermon the Master shows the importance and place of these more passive virtues of life. His disciples are not to resist evil; they are to bear scorn and blows with resignation and patience; only thus shall they show that they are indeed the children of the Father who is in heaven.

These virtues, which for want of a better name are called passive virtues receive in the life and teaching of Christ a new emphasis and importance. So long as the world is as it is, men are apt to overlook these more quiet and unobtrusive virtues. Men tell us that without courage, self-assertiveness and pride we shall not be able to maintain ourselves. Humility and meekness, patience and contentment, with many people savor of weakness and servility. But Jesus Christ knew better than we; for he took a broad outlook over the entire field of the spiritual world. From this large outlook we see that these virtues of courage and resistance have played a much smaller part in the world's progress than the world has supposed. In the name of science men have told us that the law of progress is struggle for existence with survival of the fittest. So men have imagined that they must oppose strength with strength, meet exaction by exaction, match cunning with cunning, and conquer evil by resentment. But a truer and larger view of life,—that true and large view which Jesus gives—shows the utter futility and fatuity of all this. Evil may for the moment check evil, and exaction may for the time match exaction, but they cannot exterminate evil and exaction. Tolstoi deserves the thanks of all men for calling emphatic attention to some of the neglected sayings of the Son of man. With persistent and singular force he shows the utter futility of attempting to overcome evil by evil and force by force. "According to Christ's teaching the good are the meek and longsuffering; do not resist evil by force, forgive injuries, and love their enemies; those are wicked who exalt themselves, oppress, and strive, and use force" ("The Kingdom of God is Within You," p. 243). Again: "But besides corrupting public opinion, the use of force leads men to the fatal conviction that they progress, not through the spiritual impulse which impels them to the attainment of truth and its realization in life, and which constitutes the only source of every progressive movement of humanity, but by means of violence, the very force which, far from leading men to truth, always carries them further away from it. This is a fatal error, because it leads men to neglect the chief force underlying their life—their spiritual activity—and to turn all their attention and energy to the use of violence, which is superficial, sluggish, and most generally pernicious in its action" (Ibid. p. 256).

The efficiency of these passive virtues in society cannot well be overestimated. More things are wrought by patient continuance in well-doing, and humble contentment with life, than this world supposes. A careful and profound writer has said that "the productive power of virtue is found only in virtue; under this higher and more spiritual law, we see that our proper defensive weapons, and even offensive ones, are the passive virtues. Out of the quiet endurance of the unruffled spirit there proceeds the only true spirit of conquest. . . . It is the immediate result of any kind of evil to extend itself under its own terms" (Bascom: The Words of Christ, p. 125). One day when the disciples wanted to call down fire from heaven on a village of inhospitable Samaritans, the Master told them that they had neither learned his spirit nor did they really know their own. By such means his kingdom could never be advanced one hair's breadth. When arrested in the garden he deprecated the use of violence on the part of his disciples: "They that take the sword shall perish with the sword." Anger kindles more anger, force leads to more force, resistance to evil places too much honor on resistance. The Christian disciple is called to resist steadfastly every form of evil, but he must ever remember that the weapons of his warfare are not carnal, but mighty through God in the casting down of principalities and powers, the rulers of the darkness of this world, and spiritual powers of evil in heavenly places. Christ comes to destroy the works of the devil, to conquer the world for God, and to bring in his kingdom. And he does this work, not by the might of fleets and armies, but by the gentleness of love and the power of his cross. When lifted up, he gains the power of drawing all men unto himself. Nothing disarms opposition like gentleness, as nothing conquers hate like love. James Stalker tells of a young man from the country who entered a countingroom where the daily conversation was so foul and profane that it would almost have disgraced the hulks. But a month after his arrival not a man in the place dared to utter an unchaste or profane word when he was present. And this change was wrought with hardly a syllable of reproof; it was the conquest of foulness by purity, it was darkness hiding itself before the light. The old fable of the Greeks illustrates this truth. One day the wind and the sun had a dispute as to which was the stronger. They finally decided to try their powers on a passing traveller. The wind blew in great cold blasts upon the man, tugging at his cloak and trying to wrest it from him. But the colder and harder the wind blew, the tighter the man drew the cloak in around his body. Finally the sun took its turn; it threw a warm ray down upon the man, and soon he opened his arms and before long threw off the great garment. "Arrogance and pride shut us out of the spiritual treasures of the world. . . . The blossom does not unfold itself more coyly to the warm touch of light than does the human spirit to the gentleness of the human spirit. Pride and scorn hedge up the only paths by which we can enter the kingdom of heaven as one of affection. We must find our way into the grottoes that open on the sea, when the sea is at rest. Boisterous waves will only bring shipwreck at the entrance. Especially would meekness seem to be an unsuitable virtue with which to subject the world, yet the promise is, the meek shall inherit the earth" (Bascom: ibid. p. 126).

Not only are these virtues among the most efficient in the kingdom of heaven; but they are among the most necessary in the development of character. They give coherence and balance to the soul and keep it calm and strong. Many a man is enthusiastic without being patient, and forceful without being humble. To hold one's self well in hand is the first step toward any greatness. "He that ruleth his spirit," says the wise man, "is better than he that taketh a city." The mind of man never puts forth such continuous and effective power as when it is composed and coherent. The querulous and discontented spirit is far from being the spirit of Christ. Yet many a man who is zealous and forceful is sadly lacking in patience and contentment. His whole soul is in disorder and confusion, and he never is fully master of himself or of his resources. His impatience and discontent color all he does, and make his character appear sadly defective and almost repulsive. He becomes impatient with men, unloving, uncharitable, unforgiving, and his whole life is vitiated at its very spring. It is to be noted that those whom Christ pronounces great are not such as the world esteems its great ones. Among the Gentiles those who exercise lordship over men are called kings ; and they that exercise authority upon them are called benefactors. But it shall not be so among you. But he that is greatest among you, let him be as the younger; and he that is chief, as he that doth serve.

No one can study the life and teaching of Jesus Christ without seeing how marked are the virtues of patience, meekness, trust, forgiveness. With a great work to do, with the world appealing to him for help, he is never hurried, never impatient, never confused. "Many a man will go to his martyrdom with a spirit of firmness and heroic composure, whom a little weariness or nervous exhaustion, some silly prejudice, or capricious opposition, would, for the moment, throw into a fit of vexation or ill-nature. . . . And here precisely is the superhuman glory of Christ as a character, that he is just as perfect, exhibits just as great a spirit, in little trials as in great ones. In all the history of his life we are not able to detect the faintest indication that he slips or falters. And this is the more remarkable, that he is prosecuting so great a work, with so great enthusiasm; counting it his meat and drink, pouring into it all the energies of his life. For when men have great works on hand, their very enthusiasm runs to impatience. When thwarted or unreasonably hindered, their soul strikes fire against the obstacles they meet, they worry themselves at every hindrance, every disappointment, and break out in stormy and fanatical violence. But Jesus for some reason is just as even, just as serene in all his petty vexations and hindrances, as if he had nothing on hand to do. A kind of sacred patience invests him everywhere. . . He is poor, and hungry, and weary, despised, insulted by his enemies, deserted by his friends, but never disheartened, never fretted or ruffled. . . . He does not seem to rule his temper, but rather to have none, for temper, in the sense of passion, is a fury that follows the will, as the lightnings follow the disturbing forces of the winds among the clouds, and accordingly where there is no self-will to roll up the clouds, and hurl them through the sky, the lightnings hold their equilibrium and are as though they were not" (Bushnell: "Nature and the Supernatural," p. 294). The force and beauty of these words must be sufficient justification for their quotation.

II. The Analysis of Some of These Passive Virtues.

Humility. By the men of this world humility is looked upon as a sign of weakness rather than of strength. Not even by those who profess and call themselves Christians is humility always looked upon as an essential and noble virtue. But in reality it lies at the root of all that is great and fine in Christian character. No character can build very high that has not its foundations laid deep in the virtue of humility. Humility—that means keeping one's self in the background, rejoicing when others are honored, stepping aside to make place for another. Andrew Murray is constrained to say, "Alas, how much proof there is that humility is not esteemed the cardinal virtue, the only root from which the graces can grow, the one indispensable condition of fellowship with Jesus." John the Baptist has for some months filled a large place in the eye of the Jewish nation. But before long the crowds leave him to follow another. Now comes the severest trial to which any man can be subjected. One day a few faithful disciples come to him complaining of the way men have forsaken him, and saying : "All men are following this One whom you baptized." But a glad light comes into the eyes of the Baptist as he says: "He must increase, but I must decrease. Men are leaving me to follow him ? Then my joy is fulfilled." Besides this humility of John the brave self-assertiveness of Napoleon Bonaparte is but as the dust of the balances. One day when there was a quarrel in the apostolic company over the question of who should be greatest in the Kingdom, the Master placed a little child in the midst and said : " Whosoever therefore shall humble himself as this little child, the same is greatest in the kingdom of heaven." Striking almost beyond the power of words is that incident in the upper room, in Jerusalem. After a dispute about places of honor at the table the company finally get seated, but one important act has been omitted. Each man knows what is wanted, but no man will humble himself to do the task of a menial and wash the feet of the others. We read : " Jesus knowing that the Father had given all things into his hands, and that he was come from God and went to God,"—does what ? What is the most striking thing that he can do when the Divine consciousness within him is at flood tide ? " He poureth water into a basin and began to wash the disciples' feet, and to wipe them with the towel wherewith he was girded."

Sometimes the best way to exhibit a Christian virtue is to name its contrary vice. Pride and humility are the opposites the one of the other. Pride plumes itself on some advantage that it possesses real or fancied ; it exalts itself over others and says : See how much more deserving I am than you. Arrogance and pride not only keep one out of the kingdom of heaven ; but they hedge up the only path by which one can enter.

"Heaven's gates are not so highly arched
As princes' palaces; they that enter there
Must go upon their knees."

One cannot too carefully guard his spirit against pride and arrogance. "Let him consider how all want of love, all indifference to the need, the feelings, the weakness of others; all sharp and hasty judgments and utterances, so often excused under the plea of being outright and honest; all manifestations of temper and touchiness and irritation; all feelings of bitterness and estrangement, have their root in nothing but pride, that ever seeks itself, and his eyes will be opened to see how a dark, shall I not say a devilish, pride creeps in, almost everywhere, the assemblies of the saints not excepted" (Andrew Murray: Humility). There can be no Christian greatness where humility is not.

Contentment. This signifies a mind at leisure with itself, a soul that accepts whatever comes to it without repining and without murmuring. Two things are the direct opposites of contentment: worry and ambition. "Children," said a good man to the friends gathered around his death-bed, "children, during my life I have had a great many troubles, most of which never happened." Worrying is at once one of the most unreasonable things that a man can do, as it is one of the most harmful. Dean Hodges has said in striking phrase, speaking of the anxious and nervous ways of men: "St. Martha is the patron of the women and St. Vitus of the men." Because of this, men are fretful, complaining, distracted. They come to distrust themselves, to distrust others, and to distrust God.

And *ambition*—who can adequately portray the evils and dangers of ambition? Ambition in itself may be a perfectly right thing; but the word has come to have a sinister meaning because of its almost unvarying abuse. Purpose in life is most necessary, and the desire to excel is most right. No first-rate life can be content to drift, as no high character can be formed from low aims. No man is ever better than his purest aspiration, his noblest ideal, his longest thought. But ambition, which is a desire for place and power becomes one of the most tyrannical and iniquitous things, when place and power are sought for their own sakes. The desire for place and power is one of the things most contrary to the spirit of Jesus Christ. To reign over men, to have power to command them, has for long ages been the consuming passion of men. But this love of power has been the source of untold misery among men. "If any crime," says Channing, "should be placed beyond pardon it is this." Well may Ruskin say: "Nothing is done beautifully which is done in rivalship, nor nobly which is done in pride."

On the other hand, what a blessed thing is contentment. In a spirit of restless discontent men are running hither and thither, seeking for rest, for fame, for money. They are wearing their lives out, growing old before their time, losing all joy and satisfaction in life. "Thy lot or portion in life," said the Caliph Ali, "is seeking after thee; therefore be at rest from seeking after it." "All things come round to him who waits," says the old proverb. One may be diligent in business and fervent in spirit, one may seek to excel and may be eager to do, and still be contented and happy. Contentment is at once a Christian grace and a Christian duty. More than once in Scripture we are bidden to be content with such things as we have, for God has said: "I will never leave thee, nor forsake thee." "Having food and raiment," says the apostle Paul, "let us therewith be content." Godliness with contentment we are also told is great gain. Ruskin, that keen observer, has given a most striking bit of experience showing how common is this spirit of discontent. He made a journey one day across England and noticed his fellow passengers in the train and on the stations. At Carnforth he saw the passengers crowded together in the station-shed waiting for the up train. "I did not see one, out of some twenty-five or thirty persons, tidily dressed, nor one with a contented and serenely patient look. Lines of care, of mean hardship, of comfortless submission, of gnawing anxiety, or ill temper, characterized every face." On the train he watched his fellow-travelers with some curiosity, and found the same general trace of discontent and ill temper in every face. Business men, sporting men, young women, middle-aged spinsters, all told the same story in characters more or less marked. "But the first broad sum of fact, for the sake of which I have given this diary, is that among certainly not less than some seven or eight hundred people, seen by me in the course of this day, I saw not one happy face, and several hundreds of entirely miserable ones" (Fors Clavigera, LXIX).

"*Patience* is in the estimation of some a mere drudge among the virtues; and regarded as being, if necessary, yet but servile in her character. In Scripture she is a queen, magnanimous and dignified" (W. R. Williams. Religious Progress, p. 134). Temper has been defined as nine-tenths of Christianity. Certainly it is one of the tests of a man's religion. In lower realms nine-tenths of what men call genius is simply talent for hard, persevering, patient work. The impatient man is in such a hurry to reach his goal that he defeats himself by his very eagerness. Patience is the ability to labor, to wait, to suffer calmly, hopefully. The men whose names stand high in the worlds of literature, art, science and religion, are the men who knew how to toil terribly, men who knew how to form a plan, and patiently, unfalteringly follow it for long years. Day after day they toiled on, each day adding a little to their stores of knowledge, each day writing a line, or retouching a feature, or gaining a new experience.

The impatient man lives a discontented and confused life. He is forever running against himself and thwarting himself. He becomes ill-tempered and querulous, and loses control of his powers. "Whoever is out of patience," says Lord Bacon, "is out of possession of his soul. Men must not turn bees, and kill themselves in stinging others!" "The peculiarity of ill-temper," says Professor Drummond, "is that it is the vice of the virtuous. It is often the one blot on an otherwise noble character. You know men who are all but perfect, and women who would be entirely perfect, but for an easily ruffled, quick-tempered or touchy disposition. This compatibility of ill-temper with high moral character is one of the strangest and saddest problems of ethics. . . . No form of vice, not worldliness, not greed of gold, not drunkenness itself, does more to un-Christianize society than evil temper. For embittering life, for breaking up communities, for destroying the most sacred relationships, for devastating homes, for withering up men and women, for taking the bloom off childhood, in short, for sheer, gratuitous misery-producing power, this influence stands alone." The story is told of an emperor of China, how one day passing through his dominions, he came to a house where the master and his wife, his children, and his servants all lived together in perfect harmony. The emperor was struck with admiration and inquired the means used in producing this happy result. The old man took out a pencil and wrote three words—Patience—Patience—Patience. "Patience is power," says an eastern proverb. "With time and patience the mulberry leaf becomes satin." "I have not so great struggle with my vices, great and numerous as they are," said Calvin, "as I have with my impatience. My efforts are not absolutely useless; yet I have never been able to conquer this ferocious wild beast." "It is our patience which is the touchstone of our virtue," says Amiel. No wonder the apostle Peter should place patience in the list of Christian graces between temperance and godliness.

Patience has often been travestied and counterfeited. Sometimes a stoical apathy or an affected obduracy to physical suffering has been dignified by the name of patience. Sometimes it has been made to appear as a weak indifference to all error and wickedness. The man who is meek and patient in the presence of wrong, through tameness or want of self-respect, or from fear, deserves no honor. Patience is the resolute holding in of one's self through principle; it is gentleness full of energy; it is forbearance curbing the soul's passion; it is passion subjecting itself to reason and religion. Patience is the one virtue which most truly betokens strength of character. It is not easy for a man whose soul is a flaming passion for righteousness and truth to be always calm and patient. The man who is sure of himself and sure of his cause is the man who is most patient and calm. The little boy, who knows nothing of seeds and nothing of nature's laws, digs down in the ground the next day to see what has become of the seed he planted. Jesus Christ the Great Husbandman was the most patient of men. Nothing disconcerted him, nothing discouraged him, nothing surprised him, nothing made him impatient. He knew just what to expect in this world of weak and wandering human wills. The bad and gross and foul things that mingle so inexplicably with the good ought not to be taken as a matter of course. But the Master sees these things just as they are, and takes them all into account in his plans for his kingdom. It is not easy for one who has Christ's vision to have Christ's patience. "The trouble is," said Theodore Parker, "God is not in a hurry, but I am." The beloved apostle beheld the new heavens and the new earth wherein dwells righteousness. And now, after the toil and sorrow and delay of two thousand years, men wait for the realization of that dream. "Unless the prophet shall share equally in the vision and the patience of God, he will run the earth wild, he will end in despair" (Gordon : Christ of To-Day, p. 73). Patience for life, patience in service, are quite as necessary as zeal and devotion.

Character is Christian character only in so far as it is more harmonious, more consistent, more lovable than all other character. These passive virtues may not bulk so large in the eyes of men as the more active virtues ; they may not attract so much attention as their more conspicuous and complemental virtues. But they are most necessary to the full-orbed manhood in Christ Jesus. "We no sooner forecast the future broadly, we no sooner come under the government of an omnipresent constructive idea, than we find occasion for patience, that we may not be unduly fretted by delay; for forgiveness, that we may cut short none of the forces which work for success; for meekness, that we ourselves may enter with a chastened and obedient spirit into this kingdom of harmony and love" (Bascom: The Words of Christ, p. 44). It is quite as important that Pilgrim retain his roll, as that he withstand Apollyon. To bear toil with patience, to stand and wait, to be long-suffering and forbearing with revilers, will try the temper of the finest virtue, as they will prove the touchstone of the finest character. The New Citizen, who is armed only with offensive weapons is but half armed. In the apostle's catalogue of the Christian soldier's armor the girdle of truth is as important as the sword of the Spirit; the shield of faith is as necessary as the shoes of readiness. Thus and thus only will the good soldier of Jesus Christ be perfect, thoroughly furnished unto every good work, and thoroughly prepared for every trial.

CHAPTER VII.

THE TRANSFIGURED TASK.

And whatsoever ye do in word or in deed, do all in the name of the Lord Jesus, giving thanks to God the Father through him.
The Epistle to the Colossians.

It is not the theoretical unbelief of to-day that troubles me; it is the practical ungodliness. The worst denial is not the denial of the name of God, but of the reign of God, and his reign is everywhere denied whenever men confess that he is, but live as if he had no kingdom, no law to govern the individual, to be incorporated or realized in the society or the state. Men have been too anxious to limit religion, to keep it as they think to its own province and work, forgetting that the province of religion is the whole man and the whole life of all men.—PRIN. A. M. FAIRBAIRN.

O Thou, whose love is not confined to temples made with hands, enlarge my heart to worship Thee. Help me to see Thee where men see only the world, to hear Thee where men hear only the voices of the crowd. Enlarge the range of my experience. Teach me to realize the awful solemnity of the things that I call common. Impress me with the truth that the meanest household duty is a service of Thee, that the smallest act of kindness is a praise of Thee, that the tiniest cup of water, though it were given only in a disciple's name, is a worship and a love of Thee. Help me to feel thy presence everywhere, that even in the prosaic haunts of men and in the commonplace battles of life I may be able to lift up mine eyes and say, "This is none other than the house of God, this is the gate of heaven."—GEORGE MATHESON.

SALVATION is a change of heart, before it is a change of place. The New Jerusalem is an experience before it is a home. Heaven enters the man before the man enters heaven. The eternal life and the eternal world are not future facts but present realities. The Christian life is the manifestation in time of the life of eternity. The Christian disciple who passes from death unto life passes out of the realm of the temporal and secular into the kingdom of the eternal and the sacred. He lives in the kingdom of redemption which is a present kingdom. God has become all in all to him; in God all men, all societies, all worlds live and move and have their being. He sees God in all things and all things in God. Here and now the glory of God fills the world; the light of God rests upon the city in which he dwells; the glory of God lightens every street and the presence of God transfigures every task.

The New Citizen enters into the Christian conception of life; and his life becomes the application of the Christian principle.

I. The Christian Conception of Life.

Religion, like life, has its stages of growth and development. Here, as in nature, it is first the blade, then the ear, and after that the full corn in the ear. Judaism was a divine religion so far as it went, but it was neither final nor complete. We do not expect to find a fully formed Christian conception in pre-Christian times. Judaism assumed that a part of life was sacred and holy unto God. Into the week there projected the Sabbath law in which one seventh of a man's time was claimed by Jehovah. Concerning the other six-sevenths the average Jew did not predicate much sacredness; that one-seventh was God's usually was interpreted to mean that six-sevenths were man's. The Jew could believe also that the temple was a holy place, but somehow that signified that all other places were unholy. Certain men were holy, the priests officiating at the holy altar; but the average Jew felt himself to be a very common and secular person. Whatever may have been the thought in the minds of some of the great prophets of Israel, the rank and file of the people made religion a matter of times and places and forms. Sharply drawn is the distinction between the clean and the unclean, the secular and the holy.

Jesus Christ makes all things new. Christianity fulfills and enlarges Judaism, and in a sense supersedes it. "When that which is perfect is come, then that which is in part shall be done away." Many of the old ideas and distinctions of Judaism have been superseded, swallowed up, and lost in the greater light and glory of the Christian revelation. The star of the morning is very beautiful, as it rises and shines to herald the coming of the day; but by and by the orb of day wheels up over the horizon and the light of that star fades, lost in the greater light of the rising sun. So the distinctive light of Judaism is lost in the glorious day-break of the Sun of righteousness that has risen upon the earth never to set. Several illustrations of this truth from the New Testament are sufficient to make plain the wide difference between the old and the new. One day the Lord Jesus sat by a wellside in Samaria resting while his disciples were buying bread in the neighboring village. A conversation springs up between him and a woman who comes to draw water from this ancient well. As the conversation proceeds, the woman sees that the one before her is no ordinary Jew; soon she comes to the conclusion that he is a prophet. Now she plies him with a question, an old, puzzling, divisive question, the question which separated Jew from Samaritan. Which is the proper place in which to worship God—Mount Gerizim or Jerusalem? Her question reflected the imperfect idea of religion and of worship which dominated the life and pervaded the thought of Judaism, the idea that worship performed in one place is more acceptable to God than worship in some other place; that the elements of place and time make worship acceptable or unacceptable unto God. Wonderfully significant is the reply of Jesus: "Woman, believe me, the hour cometh, when neither in this mountain, nor in Jerusalem shall ye worship the Father. God is a Spirit, and they that worship him must worship in spirit and in truth." In the light of these words the old barriers between Jew and Samaritan fade away; the distinction between the sacred and the secular disappears; in every place the soul of man may find holy ground and worship God acceptably. The old strife of men about Gerizim and Jerusalem, over clean and unclean, here and there, becomes meaningless contention. There is no place more holy than another, no city in which God is peculiarly present, no temple in which alone he is found. God is spirit, and place and time are nothing to spirit.

This truth comes out in Paul's letter to the Galatians. "But now that ye have come to know God, or rather to be known of God, how turn ye back again to the weak and beggarly rudiments whereunto ye desire to be in bondage over again? Ye observe days, and months, and seasons, and years. I am afraid of you, lest by any means I have bestowed labor upon you in vain." The old life that these Galatians had known was a life of slavery to rudiments, a life full of fear and degradation. Their gods were stern and implacable, and the worshiper was never sure that the gods were sufficiently propitiated. To these men there has come the knowledge of God in Christ Jesus; they have become partakers of his glory, and life and freedom. Yet here they are turning back to Judaism, going back into a slavery almost as bad as that from which they have been delivered. The Jewish people did not worship God in the freedom of the spirit, they remained in the bondage of forms and times and place, they supposed the divine favor to depend upon such things as the washings of pots and cups, the number of feet one walked on the Sabbath or the posture assumed in prayer. They are keeping months, and seasons, and days; they are making acceptance with God depend upon the accidents of time and place. The principle beneath all this is the principle which Jesus enunciated in all his life and teaching: the whole round of life belongs to God, and no part of it can be profane and secular and unclean. "No ceremony is of the essence of Christianity. No outward rite by itself makes a Christian" (Findlay: Galatians, The Expositor's Bible, p. 439). In Christ Jesus the middle wall of partition between God and the world is broken down, and everything is claimed by God and for God. In his letter to the Corinthians the same principle comes into view. "Whether therefore ye eat or drink, or whatsoever ye do, do all to the glory of God" (1 Cor. x. 31). Every meal is to be a real supper of the Lord, partaken in his spirit and to his glory. The Breaking of Bread observed in the church gathering on the Sunday is not the only meal eaten in remembrance of Christ and to the glory of God. The most commonplace things as eating and drinking share in the common sanctity of the Christian's life. He who truly knows God does not call anything common nor unclean. Akin to this is that other exhortation (1. Cor. vii. 20). "Let each man abide in that calling wherein he was called." There is no form of work which in itself is secular, as there is none which in itself is sacred. The man who knows God sees that life is a great and divine thing; he sees that his work in the world is a divine appointment. In becoming a Christian one does not need to change his trade in order to do Christian service, but to change his spirit. The most commonplace work may become the divinest service.

There is no room for a secular interest or an unclean thing in a world so full of God. The prophet Zechariah foretells a day when the divineness of all things shall be recognized. "In that day shall there be upon the bells of the horses HOLINESS UNTO THE LORD; and the pots in the Lord's house shall be like the bowls before the altar. Yea, every pot in Jerusalem and in Judah, shall be Holiness unto the Lord of hosts" (Zech. xiv. 20, 21). Here we have the very essence of the spirit of Christianity. In Christianity a new conception of life is given to the world; and the man who believes in Jesus Christ lives in a new world, a divine world. The old distinction between the sacred and the profane, the clean and the unclean, passes away; everything the Christian sees and touches bears the stamp of its consecration to the Lord's service. Holiness shall be introduced into the most commonplace things, even into the things once thought so very profane and common. The very harness of the horses in the street shall be holiness unto the Lord. The pots and cups in the homes of the people shall be like the bowls before the altar. The whole city in which man dwells, the great world in which he toils, is transfigured with the life of God and filled with his glory. No distinction in sacredness shall be made between the earthen pots and cups in the home and the golden cups and bowls of the temple; the work of the mechanic and the work of the preacher are equally holiness unto the Lord. The man who truly knows God sees God in everything; he cannot do one thing apart from God.

Most people feel that there is a sad division running through life. To-day, after all these centuries of Christianity, we talk of the sacred and the secular; we have our religious history and our profane history; we have our religious work and our secular duties; we have our holy days and places, and our secular days and our common places. We have our hours of devotion on the mount, when we feel that it is good to be here. But the hour passes and we must arise and go down into the world to mingle with the common and secular things of life. Somehow there comes a jar and a clash. It seems that we are living in two separate spheres and that we must divide up our allegiance between them. What is given to one side of life we feel is so much taken off the other side. I have somewhere read of a religious exquisite who said he could not buy a barrel of flour without losing a little grace by it. With many people spiritual-mindedness means an aloofness from the common affairs of life.

Now it is hardly necessary to say that this is a sad and serious mistake. A man's religion is for the sake of his life, and his business is the sphere of manifestation of his religion. A man's prayer in the church is no more religious than his transaction over the counter. Worship that means anything is a preparation for service. The work of the week is as much an act of religion as the act of kneeling in the church on Sunday. Before we know what a man's prayer and worship are worth on Sunday we must know how he lives all the week. "By their fruits ye shall know them." We observe the Lord's Day, the first day of the week as our Sabbath. It is the beginning of days to us, the token that all the week is holy unto the Lord. Sunday is only a sample of what all the week should be. The church building is a sacred house, but it is only a type of what every house in the community should be. The Lord's Supper is a sacred meal, eaten in remembrance of Christ; but it sets the standard for every other meal. Christianity is not a religion of times and places, of forms and ceremonials. They have turned their back upon Jesus Christ and have gone back into Judaism with its bondage to the law and the letter who would make it so. Sunday is a holy day; the church is a sacred building, the Lord's Supper is a holy meal, testifying forever to the fact that all other days and houses and meals are sacred and holy.

The boundary line between the secular and the sacred is not in things but in men. There is the secular, the common, the unclean, but it is not a quality of things but a matter of spirit. "To the pure, all things are pure; but to them that are defiled and unbelieving, nothing is pure." "This universe," says Robertson of Brighton, "is the express image and direct counterpart of the souls that dwell in it. Be noble-minded, and all nature replies—I am divine, the child of God; be thou, too, his child and noble. Be mean, and nature dwindles into a contemptible smallness." Sin in the heart of man turned Eden into a wilderness; holiness of heart turns the wilderness back into the garden of God. Nothing can be more alien to the spirit of Christ, nothing can be more fatal to true religion, than to call one kind of work sacred and another kind secular. Christ allows no such gulf to separate God from his world; he allows no distinction between the temple of prayer and the place of toil. In itself one kind of work may be just as sacred as another. Preaching sermons may be done in a most profane spirit, and cobbling shoes may be a most sacred service. Not the place nor the act, but the motive and the spirit give value before heaven. The roar of machinery in the mill may be a hymn of praise to God; while the surging of the church organ may be an abomination before him. Paul preached sermons and sewed tents with equal fervor and piety. Jesus was just as willing to work at the carpenter's bench as to preach the sermon on the mount. Anything that was done in honor of the Father's will was hallowed unto God. History tells of the way the old Franks had of treating their kings. They honored them, kept them in magnificent palaces, but allowed them very little authority in the everyday affairs of government. Upon special occasions the king was brought out to grace a procession or to honor some special event. But all the other days in the year the kings were kept in reverential impotence and useless idleness. That is just what many people do with their religion. They keep it for Sunday and the house of God, but all other days of the week and in all other places they manage their affairs with little reference to the glory of God or the name of Christ.

This universe, in its deepest foundations, is Christian. The Maker puts his stamp upon his work; the attributes of the Maker are manifest in all that he has made. There never has been a time when Christ was absent from creation. This is not the devil's world; it is Christ's world. Those attributes of God which we find in Christ are the moulds in which the whole creation is shaped. This universe is built on Christian principles and is held fast in the arms of Christ's love. There is an upward and Christward pressure in all things, in all plants, in all animals, all men, all societies. Christ is the source and life of creation, and creation is struggling up to behold him, to become like him, to crown him. The man who really knows Jesus Christ sees him in everything, in every plant, in every bird, in every raindrop. He finds sermons in stones, prophecies in seeds, love-messages in rain-drops, and theologies in flowers. The music of the running brook sings of him who is the soul of music; the glory of the sunset sky tells of him whose person is all glorious; the procession of the stars and the outgoings of the morning remind him of the One who is the All-orderly and whose works are all in truth.

> The world we live in wholly is redeemed;
> Not man alone, but all that man holds dear;
> His orchards and his maize, forget-me-nots
> And heartsease in his garden—all the wild
> Aerial blossoms of the untamed wood
> That make its savagery so homelike—all
> Have felt Christ's sweet love watering their roots.
> There are no gentile oaks, no pagan pines;
> The grass beneath our feet is Christian grass;
> The wayside weed is sacred unto him.

II. THE APPLICATIONS OF THIS CHRISTIAN PRINCIPLE.

Christianity is the most real and practical religion in the world. There is a sense in which we may say that it is an earth religion. Christianity is not so much the revelation of some invisible world, as a manifestation of the divine glory and the divine power in this present world. Jesus Christ has come to transmute and transfigure the dust of our humanity into the righteousness and glory of the living God.

With this Christian conception of life throbbing in his heart, the Christian citizen rises in the morning and goes about his daily tasks. His eye is full of the light of the glory of God, and he sees the light and glory of God filling everything and transfiguring everything. He sees that his work in the world is a divine calling; his occupation is the vantage ground from which he reaches forth in service of his fellows. The man who has entered into the secret and meaning of the Christian life sees that his work is given him by divine appointment. He hears Paul say, "Paul, an apostle by the grace of God." And he says just as devoutly, "I, a shoemaker by the grace of God. I, a merchant by the grace of God. I, a manufacturer by the grace of God. I, a miner by the grace of God. I, a farmer by divine calling.

When did Jesus begin to do the Father's will? The moment we think of it, every one must say there never was a time when he was not about the Father's business. Jesus working at the carpenter's bench was doing the will of God as truly as when preaching the sermon on the mount. A table made by his hands would bear the same marks of divine sonship as the sermon on the mount. Suppose we had some article of furniture which, it is claimed, was made by the Carpenter of Nazareth, a table or chair. There seems no question about its authenticity; the hand that was nailed to the cross made this table. Reverently we turn it over, noting carefully the workmanship. We find that it is a plain table, and is somewhat rudely finished, owing no doubt to the rude and imperfect tools with which he worked. But by and by, we come to a defect in the workmanship; we find that three legs are properly mortised and joined, but the fourth is only glued in place, in imitation of a mortise. In surprise, we look up and ask, Who made this table? For reply we are told, Jesus of Nazareth. Who was this Jesus of Nazareth? we further ask. He was the Son of God, the sinless man, the Teacher and Saviour of men. Well, then, he did not make this table; for the man who made it was not even a good man. Either Jesus was not a good man, or he did not make this table. We know how the Master prayed to the Father, how he preached the sermon on the mount, how he opened the eyes of the blind, and how he finally died as a sacrifice for men on the cross. Then we conclude that he did not make this table. But we are assured he did; generations of men have attributed it to him. Well, it does not matter what tradition says: He did not make this table; the man who made it was not a good man, not an honest workman; look at this piece of dishonest, scamped work. No amount of evidence would be sufficient to authenticate such a table as that. Since Jesus was here in the world to reveal God, to glorify the Father, his whole life, from beginning to end, was a divine service. In a word, Jesus Christ, by his life on earth, has shown the divineness of all life, and the glory of all work.

Paul made tents and preached sermons with equal fervency. Some of his letters and sermon notes have come down to us, and the world has called these inspired writings. Suppose we had a piece of tent-cloth made by his hand. That tent-cloth would bear the same water-marks of inspiration that his letters bear. A bit of intentionally dishonest or careless sewing from Paul's hand would invalidate every one of his letters and brand him as a fraud. The principle is plain : a man's work from day to day is the sphere in which his Christian life shows itself. The man who does dishonest work on Monday cannot make an honest prayer on Sunday. The mechanic who scamps his work scamps his religion. The Christian spirit cannot work in a vacuum. The Christianity of Christ demands that the whole life be lived out under the direct dominion of the Son of man and in fulfillment of his spirit. Christianity has its mysteries which reach away up beyond the stars, clear to the very throne of God. But, for all that, it is the religion of everyday life and of commonplace duties. It has to do with real and human things, with such real and human things as eating and drinking, buying and selling, voting and working ; it is the religion of the store, the home, the church, the street, the hall of legislation, the counting-room. Never think of Christianity as something apart from life, something added on to life, some special accomplishment, as music or painting. Religion, the religion of the Son of man, is not a thing of times and places, of cloisters and closets, not a thing of raptures and sentiments, of opinions and feelings, but of downright, outright determination to honor the will of God in everything one does. "Without human life to act upon," says

Professor Drummond, "without the relations of men with one another, of master with servant, husband with wife, buyer with seller, creditor with debtor, there is no such thing as Christianity." The daily round of life is the sphere of manifestation of the Christian principle.

> We need not bid for cloister'd cell
> Our neighbor and our work farewell,
> Nor strive to wind ourselves too high
> For sinful man beneath the sky.
>
> The trivial round, the common task,
> Would furnish all we ought to ask:
> Room to deny ourselves; a road
> To bring us, daily, nearer God.—KEBLE: *Morning.*

The Christianity of Christ claims all life for God. Many of those who profess and call themselves Christian disciples have never yet entered into this primary truth of the gospel. They think and live as if great provinces of life lay outside the boundaries of God's kingdom. They regret with a deep and sincere regret that so much of life should be taken up with what they call the secular affairs of life. Men and women, hard-working, faithful, busy people look upon their daily tasks as a kind of desert region in which the fair fruits of the Christian life cannot be expected to thrive. They look upon that real world in which nearly all their time is spent, as an evil world, a world given over to the prince of the power of the air, but a world in which they must toil and live. No mistake could be more tragic, more contrary to the spirit of Christianity than this. Whatever we do, in word or in deed, we are to do all in the name of the Lord Jesus. Spirituality is not a zone of life, but a tone of thought. One man may be wholly unspiritual in the church, and another may be wholly spiritual in the mill. The fact is, however, everything in life is essentially spiritual. The relations of parent, child, husband, wife, brother, sister, friend, neighbor, associate, are throughout "every living tie and thrilling nerve that binds them together" essentially spiritual relations. The simplest relations of life and the most commonplace acts have a spiritual significance. Here, in this earthly scene, here, amid the throng and press of daily cares, here, in these shops, and streets, and homes, the Christian Citizen must live and serve; here, fidelity is tested, character is made, spirituality is shown.

Let me put this truth in a different way. You are a business man: your calling in life is to infuse the Christian spirit into the commercial world, and to place the crown of the business world upon the head of Jesus Christ. You are a mechanic: your calling in life is to work with God in the creation of order and beauty, and to imitate the Carpenter of Nazareth in glorifying God in daily toil. You are a farmer: your calling is to see God in the processes of nature and to be a link in the chain of divine providence in feeding hungry men. You are a housewife: your calling is to spiritualize the relations of the home and make the family life below the shadow of the family above. You are a director in a great corporation : your calling in life is to honor Jesus Christ in the affairs of that company, in its issuing of stock and its payment of employés, and to show that love, not selfishness, is the glory of trade. You are a lawyer : your calling in life is to interpret the righteousness of God written upon the Adamant Tables, and to show that all human relations are rooted in justice. Mohammed has said in striking phrase : " One hour spent in the execution of justice is worth seventy years of prayer." To be a Christian and to serve one's day and generation one does not need to change his calling or work in life, unless that business is clearly wrong. Often the best thing is to remain right in the calling wherein he is called and to ennoble and spiritualize it. Men, most men want to be useful : they want to serve their fellows according to the will of God. The world needs Christian preachers and missionaries : but often the most effectual preacher in a community is the merchant who spiritualizes trade and makes his counter an altar of service. It is a fine and Christly thing to crucify self and become a missionary to lost men in some other land. But it is equally as fine and Christly a thing to disown self in the store and to honor the law of the cross over one's counter. Perhaps the best way in which the average disciple can most effectually honor Christ is remaining in the calling wherein grace found him, and seeking to infuse the Christian spirit into every relation and into every transaction. That is a suggestive page in one of Ruskin's letters, wherein he speaks of a visit to the home of St. Francis of Assisi. "It is not at all clear to me how far the Beggar and Pauper Saint, whose marriage with the Lady Poverty, I have come here to paint from Giotto's dream of it,— how far, I say, the mighty work he did in the world was owing to his vow of poverty, or diminished by it. If he had been content to preach love alone, whether among poor or rich, and if he had understood that love for all God's creatures was one and the same blessing : and that if he was right to take the doves out of the fowler's hand, that they might build their nests, he was himself wrong when he went out in the winter's night on the hills, and made for himself dolls of snow, and said, 'Francis, these—behold—these are thy wife and thy children.' If instead of quitting his father's trade, that he might nurse lepers, he had made his father's trade holy and pure, and honorable more than beggary : perhaps at this day the Black Friars might yet have an unruined house by Thames shore, and the children of his native village not be standing in the porches of the temple built over his tomb to ask alms of the infidel" (Fors Clavigera, Letter XLI.).

The Christian is here not to despise the world nor to destroy the world, but to hallow and transfigure the world. This is God's world, and it is the privilege of the Christian disciple to see God in everything and to put the stamp of God upon everything. The religion that makes one hold lightly the relations of life is not Christ's kind of religion. The religion that does not sweeten the home, sanctify the store, transform the mill, purify politics, is not Christ's kind of religion. The Christian Citizen has a divine calling to spiritualize the secular and to Christianize the common. When this principle dominates the life, all work becomes one round of holy service. Then one need not lay down the broom or close the ledger and enter the closet to find holy ground. When Christ has full sway in the life, every place becomes a place of prayer, every task an altar of service, every spot an open gate of heaven, every duty a spiritual exercise, every street a street of the New Jerusalem.

> Teach me, my God and King,
>   In all things thee to see ;
> And what I do in anything,
>   To do it as for thee.
>
> All may of thee partake ;
>   Nothing so small can be,
> But draws when acted for thy sake,
>   Greatness and worth from thee.
>
> If done beneath thy laws,
>   Even servile labors shine ;
> Hallowed is toil, if this the cause ;
>   The meanest work Divine.

A servant with this clause
   Makes drudgery divine;
Who sweeps a room, as for thy laws
   Makes that and the action fine.—
                    GEORGE HERBERT.

CHAPTER VIII.

THROUGH VANITY FAIR.

They that use this world, as not abusing it.—THE APOSTLE PAUL.

Our fathers delivered the holy land from the infidel. There is another holy land which brigands, thieves, the profane, pollute every day. It is the land of laughter and of pleasure. They have so thoroughly ravaged and disfigured it that it is not recognizable. But by the God of the springtime and of the stars, by the loving kindness which gives the fresh laugh to the lips of childhood and the sweet intoxication to the heart of youth, this holy land of ours shall not remain in the hands of infidels. It is ours and we shall regain it.—CHARLES WAGNER: *Youth.*

> The toppling crags of duty scaled,
> Lie close upon the shining table lands
> To which our God himself is sun and moon.
> —ANON.

IN Bunyan's immortal allegory we are told how, as Pilgrim proceeds on his journey, he is met by his good friend Evangelist, who warns him against over-confidence. "Then I saw in my dream that when they were gone out of the wilderness, they presently saw a town before them, and the name of that town is Vanity: and at the town there is a fair kept, called Vanity Fair. It is kept all the year long. It beareth the name of Vanity Fair, because the town where it is kept is lighter than vanity; and also because all that is there sold or that cometh thither is vanity." Here the Christian Pilgrims are hardly treated, and Faithful is killed. But he who ruleth all things, with the temptation made a way of escape for Christian, so that he is delivered from the snares of the city and goes on his way singing.

Vanity Fair is a perennial and permanent institution in every community on earth. As the New Citizen passes to and fro, from his work to his home, and from his home to the church, he passes through the streets of this fair. . As he goes from the Prayer Room to the Palace Beautiful he sees the placards and announcements of this seductive fair. In the place of toil and in the social gathering he meets the agents of this wonderful fair, who ever seek to interest him in its allurements. "As I said, the way to the Celestial City lies just through this town where this lusty fair is kept; and he that would go to the City, and yet not go through this town, must needs go out of the world." That fair represents the pleasures, the attractions, the allurements, the temptations of this world. Bunyan is right, beyond question; he who would go to the City and not go through this town must needs go out of the world. Even the Prince of princes himself went through this town on his way to his own country, and that on a fair day. Dropping the allegory we now ask: How shall the Christian disciple who would be true, conduct himself amid the allurements, the distractions, the pleasures, the seductions of this world? Shall he despise the world and all its honors and attractions? Shall he love these things and give himself up to the enticements of the fair? Is there a possible third course, which consists neither in despising the world nor in loving the world, but in using the world as not abusing it? One cannot pass through the world without passing through Vanity Fair; can one pass through this fair without being seduced from his integrity and spoiled in his devotedness?

I. THE CHRISTIAN CITIZEN MAY ENJOY LIFE WHILE PASSING THROUGH THE WORLD.

Though the disciple must preserve his integrity while passing through Vanity Fair, he need not deny himself all pleasure and enjoyment in life. On no question is information more needed than this of the right attitude of the Christian toward the pleasures and recreations of the world. "There are three classes of individuals," says Charles Wagner in *Youth*, "who disapprove of pleasure. There are, doubtless, more than three, but to enumerate them all would be to do them too much honor. It would be as dreary as a succession of rainy days. Three will suffice,—utilitarians, ascetics, and pessimists." The first, as he shows, proscribe pleasure because it is useless, and makes us lose time without any equivalent. The second condemn pleasure because it is dangerous in their eyes and jeopardizes the soul's salvation. And the third class, the pessimists, deny pleasure because it deranges their system, and does not frame in with their little theory of the world and of life. No one of these views is fully satisfactory, because none is fully Christian.

Long ago Aristotle laid down the maxim that " All extremes are wrong." What may be called the ascetic view of life has more or less prevailed in all ages. Men, earnest men, have seen the follies of the world and have felt the attractions of society. In their recoil from these things they have gone to the length of denying the validity of all pleasure ; they have preached forever and forever the duty of utter abstinence, of total isolation from the world and its attractions. It may be granted that asceticism and puritanism have had an important part to play in the drama of the world's development ; they were protests against that view of life which made it consist in one round of fun and frolic. In the name of religion, men have been cruel to themselves, and have denied themselves all earthly joy and recreation. Vice and pleasure have been placed in the same category. We have heard much of the strictness of the Puritans, and no doubt they were somewhat ascetic and gloomy in their views of life. In their protest against the follies and vices of the time of the Stuarts they went to extremes. There is some justification for the remark of Macaulay, that the Puritans objected to bear baiting, not because it gave pain to the bear, but because it gave pleasure to the spectators. They denounced all public and private amusements as sinful and demoralizing. Some of them considered it a sin to laugh on Sunday, a sacrifice of one's integrity ever to be pleased and happy. They questioned the saintliness of a man with plenty of color in his face, with a happy, ringing voice, with a healthy appetite and a good digestion; the man who had a cheerful disposition and a buoyant spirit they suspected of being wanting in some of the more serious and necessary graces of the Christian life. Even such a sane and saintly man as good Archbishop Leighton said: "Pleasures are like mushrooms—it is so difficult to distinguish those that are wholesome from those that are poisonous, that it is better to abstain from them altogether."

Christianity is not a fast but a feast. A characteristic Gospel word is "joy." Jesus Christ lived a joyous and happy life, eating and drinking and making himself at home amid the common joys of men. He was indeed the Man of Sorrows, one acquainted with grief; but he was also the Friend and Companion of man in all his joys and pleasures. An old tradition says that he was never seen to smile. One cannot reconcile this tradition with the fact that little children were drawn to him as by some mighty magnetism. A smile and not a frown wins the little child.

John the Baptist was an ascetic, living a hard and strict life in the wilderness, standing aloof from the common joys of men. No one would ever have thought of inviting him to share the joys of a marriage occasion; as he would never have thought, for one moment, of accepting such an invitation, had it been given. But no doubt it seemed the most natural and becoming thing in the world to invite Jesus of Nazareth. And he honored the occasion by his presence and wrought his first miracle to minister to the joys of the hour. He came eating and drinking; he lived the common life of men; there was outwardly nothing remarkable in his life or dress or conduct; there were no outward and visible marks of eminent religiousness. We know how the Pharisees and the disciples of John were surprised and hurt by this; they did not see how one could be religious without being ascetic and self-denying in such things as dress and worship, eating and drinking. "Wisdom is justified of her children," he said to all cavillers. "I am come that they might have life and that they might have it more abundantly." Abundant life shows itself not in abundant dreaming, nor in abundant renouncing, but in abundant living and enjoying.

Pleasure and recreation are a necessity of life. That is an interesting tradition of John the beloved disciple, how one day, while amusing himself with a tame partridge, a huntsman expressed wonder that he could spend time in so unprofitable a manner. The apostle inquired: "Why dost thou not carry thy bow always bent?" "Because if it were always bent I fear it would lose its spring, and become useless." "Be not surprised, therefore," replied the saintly disciple, "that I should sometimes remit a little of my close attention of spirit to enjoy a little recreation, that I may afterwards employ myself more fervently in divine contemplation." Men are so constituted that periods of work must interblend with periods of rest and recreation. "All work and no play makes Jack a dull boy." "There is a time to weep," says the wise man, "and a time to laugh." There is a laughter that is like the crackling of thorns under a pot; but there is a laughter which is the joyous overflow of a full soul. Carlyle with his keen insight has said: "Beware of the man who cannot laugh." "The man who cannot laugh is not only fit for treasons, stratagems, and spoils, but his whole life is already a treason and a stratagem." "I love honest laughter as I do sunlight." Perhaps one of the most important elements of Luther's work is his influence upon the daily life of men. He preached a gospel of joyousness and peace. As Dale has said: "He had a boundless faith and a boundless joy in God. His joy was of a masculine kind, and made him stronger for his work." He was a hearty eater and enjoyed seeing his friends at dinner eating and enjoying themselves. He married a wife and loved her, and loved God all the more for it. He was exceedingly fond of music and songs, and he could laugh as well as preach.

The discussion of this whole question of amusement needs to be treated in a high and Christian spirit. Too often the whole discussion turns on the propriety or the danger of certain forms of pleasure, as theater-going, card-playing, and dancing. To reject is easier than to discriminate; to lay down rules is simpler than to set forth principles. To lay down rules may be easy, but it is neither wise nor Christian. The Christian gospel is not a system of rules and restrictions, but a high inspiration, a principle of life. To frame the life by principles and inspirations is at once to develop character and to honor the Christian spirit. One of the most painful sights in the world is to see a young man debating anxiously whether he may engage in this amusement or that recreation. He whose religion is a matter of rules and restrictions so debates; he who lives by principles and inspirations cultivates an insight which becomes quick to discern between the right and the wrong. Character consists in the development of insight. Austin Phelps says that "the most senseless advice he ever heard was that given by a Christian father to his son: "I do not say pro or con about card-playing; but it must not be practiced in my house." It is not surprising, says Phelps, that the boy went to sea. The real education of life comes not through keeping rules but through applying principles.

A few principles for the guidance of life may be given. I pass by all such considerations as the rightfulness or wrongfulness of some of the common forms of amusement of our time. I lay down no general and sweeping prohibitions; I pass by all questions of casuistry and debate. A few general principles, negatively and positively, are here given.

I. NEGATIVELY.

1. All forms of amusement are to be avoided which tend to undermine or endanger one's physical health. Any forms of recreation which rob one of sleep cannot well be justified on any grounds. So also those forms of recreation which exhaust one's physical energy unduly, and unfit one for the stern and real work of life, are questionable. Recreation, to be real and helpful, ought to send one back to his work with glowing cheeks and bounding pulse.

2. Those forms of amusement are to be avoided whose associations are questionable. Many forms of popular amusement are conducted in questionable places, by questionable methods, by questionable persons, and for questionable ends. No one who has a fine and high regard for his personal integrity can consent to be a party to questionable ways and deeds. Just so far as our presence at such places recognizes and encourages these questionable practices we had better abstain. Better that we pluck out the right eye or cut off the right hand, than by our presence to become a stumbling-block to some weaker brother.

3. Those forms of amusement are to be shunned

which arouse and stimulate a morbid desire and appetite. One cannot too carefully watch the springs of life; out of the heart are the issues of life. You have seen the storm cloud gather on a summer's day. As you look up at the blue and cloudless sky, you see a thin film and vapor gather and float lazily across the heavens. Now a breath of wind catches it, and it seems about to dissolve and disappear. In a minute you look again, and now the haze has become a cloud. While you look it grows and thickens and spreads over the face of the whole sky. Before long the heavens are black; now the lightnings flash and the thunders roll. Look within the heart, and every one will see the same process there. The book may be fascinating, but if it suggests evil imaginations, it cannot be too rigidly avoided. The place of amusement may be brilliant and attractive, but if it paints evil pictures upon the walls of the soul, it cannot be too carefully shunned.

4. Those forms of amusement are to be avoided which tend to become stumbling-blocks in the way of others. It is possible that one may himself indulge in these things without harm. But "none of us lives to himself, and none dies to himself." Every man is responsible for his influence. The apostle has laid down the principle which should guide men always and everywhere: "It is good neither to eat flesh, nor to drink wine, nor anything whereby thy brother stumbleth, or is offended, or is made weak" (Romans xiv. 21).

II. POSITIVELY.

1. All forms of amusement to be Christian must be means to an end. So far as recreation is made an end in itself it soon palls on the taste, and leaves a bitter taste in the mouth. Well has the apostle written: "She that liveth in pleasure is dead while she liveth." A soul sodden with pleasure is already a lost soul.

2. Those forms of amusement are to be preferred which minister to the higher parts of man's nature "De gustibus non est disputandum." What is one person's delight is another's abomination. No strict, hard and fast rule can be laid down as to what is higher and lower. But it may be said that the mind is higher than the body, and the spiritual appetencies are higher than bodily sensations. Grecian mythology tells of Gryllus, a companion of Ulysses, who was first feasted by Circe and then transformed into a hog. Ulysses obtained a charm by which he was enabled to restore all these swine back to men again. But one man, Gryllus, refused to resume his former shape. Fenelon has produced a profound and witty dialogue between Ulysses and Gryllus. *Ulysses:* "If you had any feeling at all, you would be only too happy to become a man again." *Gryllus:* "I don't care for that. The life of a hog is much pleasanter." *Ulysses:* "Are you not shocked at your baseness? You live only on filth." *Gryllus:* "What does it matter? Everything depends upon one's taste." *Ulysses:* "Is it possible that you have so soon for-

gotten every noble and advantageous gift of humanity?" *Gryllus:* "Do not talk to me of humanity; its nobility is only imaginary." *Ulysses:* "But you count then as nothing, eloquence, poetry, music, science, etc?" *Gryllus:* "My temperament as a hog is so happy that it raises me above all those fine things. I like better to grunt than to be eloquent in your way." So long as a man lives only in the basement of his brain he will be content with base pleasures. The man who has a high and worthy appreciation of the grandeur and dignity of human life will prefer those pleasures which minister to his higher nature.

3. Those forms of diversion are to be commended which increase the joyousness of life and add no sorrow. Men cannot too carefully avoid those forms of pleasure which give "a moment's joy to wail a week." Men, it has been said, cannot too rigidly shun those deeds by day which destroy their peace of soul by night. This is what Paul means when he says: "Happy is he that judgeth not himself in that which he approveth. But he that doubteth is condemned if he eat, because he eateth not of faith; and whatsoever is not of faith is sin."

Happy is that man whose eye is single and whose insight is clear; happy is he who does and allows only those things which his insight approves.

4. Those forms of diversion are to be encouraged which awaken in man a true appreciation of the beauties of the world and the handiwork of

God. Nature, the wonderful and many-leaved book of God, is ever new and ever beautiful. Why will men be content to shut themselves up in narrow, close rooms over cards and games when the wonderful book of nature invites them to come and read! There are certain pleasures which elevate and ennoble the soul—music, art, poetry, natural science.

"Religion never was designed to make our pleasures less." The story is told of Carlo Borromeo, a saintly man, that one day, while engaged with some friends at a game of chess, the question was started what they would do if it were known that they were to die within the hour. "I would go on with my game," said Borromeo, who had begun the game for God's glory in order to fit himself for God's work. Religion will give one some clear and sufficient principles by which to test pleasures; it will give one a spirit that will lead him into the enjoyment of true and helpful and elevating pleasures. No one who has a regard for his higher life can refuse to try the spirits of pleasure that he may know whether they be of God or not. The man who brings every pleasure to the test of his insight and the principles of the gospel cannot fail to know with a certainty that cannot be gainsaid what forms of diversion are lawful and expedient for him.

II. The Christian Citizen must Preserve his Integrity while Passing through Vanity Fair.

The sphere of manifestation of the Christian spirit is the common round of daily life. Whether we like it or not, we are in the world and cannot escape from the world. The divine Master has set his people right in the streets and fields and homes of earth, and has bidden them stay there and serve there till he calls them away to another world and a different order. On the other hand, the Christian is bidden to come out from the world and to be separate. This separation is, however, one of spirit and not of locality. "I pray not that thou shouldest take them out of the world, but that thou shouldest keep them from the evil." No one knew better than the Lord Jesus the power of temptation and the subtlety of the tempter's snare. He knew the charms of Ephesus, the fascinations of Athens, the intoxications of Rome, the hindrances of Jerusalem. Never was it harder to keep clean and true and earnest and faithful than in these wondrously intoxicating cities. But Jesus Christ expected men and women to live brave true lives right in the midst of all these temptations and seductions. The disciples in Antioch and Jerusalem, in Corinth and Ephesus, in Smyrna and Rome had no call to leave these cities for the solitary cell or the desert home. The tried and tempted disciples in Sardis and Smyrna must win the white robe and the crown of life in these cities and not in the hermit's cell. "Christ evidently believed that a man could be a Christian anywhere." The Christian must learn the art of being faithful everywhere. The Christian must learn to be a Christian anywhere and everywhere, at all times and under all circumstances.

Nothing occasions an observer of human life more surprise and sorrow than the different ways that some persons act in different surroundings. Many people allow themselves to be moulded and shaped by the influences at work around them. They are little else than the expression and reflection of their surroundings. They take the course of life that has the most supporters, or that offers the least resistance. A suggestive writer, in a little book on "Possibilities," says that nothing so surprised and dismayed his heart as the laxity of principle which he so often saw in persons as they passed from one set of surroundings to another. The man who was pure and good in America was not necessarily pure and good in France or in Turkey. A woman whose religious observances were most careful in Massachusetts was so absorbed in sight-seeing in Germany that religious observances had no place in her conduct. It is matter of common observation that persons who are regardful of the proprieties of life at home are lax even to levity at the sea-shore. "It almost seemed as though what we call Christian principle was a thing of clothes, to be put on like a fur coat when the weather was cold and to be taken off like that fur coat when the weather was warm."

Modern science has had much to say about the influence of environment on the organism. Some would tell us that man is simply the product of surroundings : that climate, food, natural scenery parentage, conditions and associates shape the life and determine the destiny of the human being. Beyond question these things do influence immeasurably and irrevocably for weal or woe the life of man. But when the story of man's environment is all told, his life-story is but half told. Another factor enters into the computation which determines the final result. This fatalistic, materialistic mould of thought is the foe of all high aspiring and noble striving. It is sadly true that these unworthy theories find their justification in the lives of a great many people. The jelly fish has very little to do with the making of its own destiny. It rises and falls on the water and is cast upon the shore at the caprice of wind and wave. But man is not a jelly-fish, at least he ought not be. Robert Browning is not creating an impossible and improbable character in Pompilia, who, like the lily in a horse pond, becomes a pure and noble soul in the most adverse surroundings. Well might the Pope say :

"It was not given Pompilia to know much,
  Speak much, to write a book, to move mankind,
  Be memorized by who records my time.
  Yet if in purity and patience, if

In faith held fast despite the plucking fiend,
Safe like the signet stone with the new name
That saints are known by,—if in right returned
For wrong, most pardon for worst injury,
If there be any virtue, any praise,—
Then will this woman-child have proved—who knows?
Just the one prize vouchsafed unworthy me,
Seven years a gardener of the untoward ground
I till,—this earth, my sweat and blood manure,
All the long day that barrenly grows dusk:
At least one blossom makes me proud at eve
Born 'mid the briars of my enclosure!"

The force of wind and tide are potent forces in this world, and do much to determine the direction of the drift and flotsam. But they do not determine the direction of the vessel manned by a brave and resolute captain. He never thinks of fastening up the helm, unshipping the oars, and letting his boat be blown and carried about whither wind and tide wish. That a man should make shipwreck of faith we can somewhat appreciate; for the world is full of mysteries and there is no clear vision. That a man should go down in the hour of temptation we can readily understand; for we have all felt the hot rush of blood in our veins. But that a man should be content to drift, that he should have no fixed harbor in view, that he should let chance make him a man if chance would have him a man—this is one of those contradictions of human nature which puzzle us.

The Christian disciple must pass through Vanity Fair on his way to the new life. But that is no reason why he should adopt the ways of the Fair and do as the world does. Here is a man who is hard, licentious and godless. How does he explain his life? "When I was a boy I had few attractions at home, and so I was compelled to seek them elsewhere. As I grew up, I naturally broke away from the restraints of home. When I went into business, I found myself beset with all kinds of evil influences. I have made shipwreck of life, but the hard, wicked selfish world has made me just what I am." So men live, and so they blame the world for the life which they themselves have made. "My companions all danced and played cards," says the young man, "and I could not well do differently." "Other men in my line of business follow certain methods," says the merchant, "and of course I must do as they do." "I know that society is more or less frivolous and shallow and worldly," says the society leader, "but as I am in society, I must conform more or less to the ways of society." So people go through the world blaming the moulds in which they voluntarily run their lives for the shape their lives take. How gentle we would be were we never provoked! How religious if we lived in a different community! How successful had we but half a chance! We would be devoted if we had any encouragement, and noble if we had any incitement. What different people we would be if the world were different! Thus it is that many a man's life is a complaint when it should be a battle. The man charges up his moral backwardness to the account of society when God charges it up to his own self-indulgent temper. Many a man spends far more time in excusing his short-comings than in reforming his life.

In all ages men have raised the cry: "It was the world that ruined us." "It was the city with its allurements that turned me astray." "It was society with its seductions that undermined my consecration! It was the school, it was the store, it was my companions, it was Vanity Fair that ruined my soul! So men cry, as they review their lives and try to justify themselves. No, it was not the store, nor the society, nor the city, nor Vanity Fair that ruined them; it was their own complaisant temper. Joseph in the house of Potiphar was tried as few men are tried. But he did not think of yielding and then shifting the responsibility on some one else. "How can I do this great wickedness and sin against God?" There was Nehemiah the leader of the returned exiles. His predecessors, the governors appointed by the Persian king, had long been in the habit of making personal gain out of the office. "So did not I because of the fear of God." Daniel and his three companions had many things against them in Babylon; they were but boys away from home, at a luxurious and dissolute court, with every inducement on the side of laxity and license. But they purposed in their hearts that they would not defile themselves with the king's meat and drink.

"We had to pass through Vanity Fair, and we lost our integrity and our zeal." But Jesus Christ allows nothing for such excuses. He is compassion itself; he has been tempted in all points even as we are, and he knows how to enter into our experiences. But he expected that his follower could be faithful anywhere and everywhere. He knew how strong was the love of the world; he knew how hard it was to endure persecution; he knew how trying it was to live in a highly intoxicated atmosphere. Yet he expected men and women to go into these cities of his time and live pure, devoted, heavenly lives. Right through Vanity Fair he expected his disciples to go without losing one particle of their love and purity and devotedness. Men and women by the hundreds and thousands have been ruined by these things; but Jesus Christ expected his followers to remain unstained and uncontaminated.

The most dangerous, the most pernicious idea that can possess one is the idea that one cannot be expected to maintain his integrity in certain circumstances. The parent who gives place to that idea in his training of his child has ruined his child. The child who enters life with that idea in his mind is hopelessly ruined. Such a conception of life is a lie, a cheat, a delusion. There is no reason for it in Scripture, in history, in everyday life. "They can conquer who believe they can."

CHAPTER IX.

IN MILL AND MARKET.

Not slothful in business.—THE APOSTLE PAUL.

A man's daily labor is the chief element in determining his character. It is by this he serves, and by this he grows. It is substantially his life, to be begun and ended, day by day, in the name of God.—BROOKE FOSS WESTCOTT.

In the eye of the Christian Founder the true city of God is a city of spiritual commerce. Each is weak where his brother is strong; each is strong where his brother is weak. Each gives to the other that special kind of riches in which the other is poor; and from the mutual interchange of strength there at length emerges a perfect Divine Republic, a city which hath foundations whose builder and maker is God.—GEORGE MATHESON.

IT is a commonplace of Christian thought that the world was designed for man. For him clouds gather and rain falls; for him the earth is clothed with beauty and the hills are stored with treasure; the long ages of change and delay were preparing a dwelling place for him. At the foot of man the world of nature lays its crown, and says: I am thine. Man is at once the crown of creation, and the final cause of creation. His original charter of sovereignty is given him by the Creator of all. "And God said, Behold, I have given you every herb yielding seed, which is upon the face of all the earth, and every tree, in which is the fruit of the tree yielding seed " (Gen. i. 29). To the same high thought spoke the Psalmist :

> Thou madest him to have dominion over the works of thy hands ;
> Thou hast put all things under his feet ;
> All sheep and oxen,
> Yea, and the beasts of the field ;
> The fowl of the air, and the fish of the sea,
> And whatsoever passeth through the paths of the sea.
> —(*Psalm*, viii. 6–8.)

But not for the sake of man's life alone is the earth given and the sovereignty conferred. It is for the sake of his soul life, in a word for the sake of moral character. God values moral character beyond all else. It is the only thing that has real and intrinsic value. And things are so arranged in this world that moral character may be made and trained. To show the relation of trade and labor to moral character is the purpose of this chapter.

I. The Moral Significance of Trade.

Those relations and interests, which for convenience we group under the name of Trade and Business, have a high moral significance. The world of things has in itself no moral character ; things are neither good nor bad ; they have, however, moral significance because they produce moral and spiritual results in living creatures. Trade and Business have ends beyond themselves.

There is a final cause of Commerce and Labor, and that is moral character.

Work is a part of man's normal condition in this world. Men have sometimes spoken as if labor was the penalty of man's sin. No doubt the presence of sin, with all that it implies, has made man's work far more hard and exhausting than it otherwise would have been. But for man, sinless or sinful, work is a part of the divine plan. Open the book of Genesis and read : " And God blessed them, and God said unto them, Be fruitful, and multiply, and replenish the earth, and subdue it : and have dominion over the fish of the sea, and over the fowl of the air, and over every living thing that moveth upon the earth " (Gen. i. 28). Man is charged to subdue the earth and to have dominion over it, and this charge antedates the beginning of sin. There is not the least shadow of intimation that work itself is a part of the curse. To be sure after sin is done, his work becomes more difficult; now he must eat bread in the sweat of his brow; but work itself is not a curse but a blessing.

The duty of labor is solemnly laid upon man in the moral law of God. In the Fourth Commandment is the charge : "Six days shalt thou labor and do all thy work." Many people, it is to be suspected, overlook this part of the commandment, and interpret it as if it had to do throughout with rest. According to the law of God in the Old Testament and in the New, it is as wrong for a man to be idle as for him to be dishonest, or impure, or covetous. Idleness is an immoral thing; an idle man is not a good man. "If any will not work, neither let him eat" (2 Thess. iii. 10). The Lord Jesus protested to the Jews: "My Father worketh hitherto and I work." No man who has understood the meaning and value of life desires to escape work.

From the past we have inherited a false conception of the duty and dignity of work. Among the peoples of antiquity, with hardly an exception, work was despised and the laborer was regarded as an inferior creature. Egypt is one of the oldest nations of which we have authentic record, and the condition of the laborer in that land was most pitiable. The people generally were slaves, without rights, without religion, without hope. The pyramids are monuments of human cruelty, built, as they were, by the enforced labor of thousands of slaves, who toiled without reward and died without regret. Throughout the East, in Assyria, Persia, Babylonia, and Phœnicia, work was despised and was performed by the slave class. The Jews had a higher conception of work than the other nations; and every Jewish boy was expected to learn a trade. In Greece and Rome, from the earliest times, slavery was known, and where slavery prevails work is lightly regarded. In Greece the philosophers, with hardly an exception, despised work and relegated it to the slave class. Plato's words are terrible in their scorn whenever he refers to the mechanical arts. In the Republic he calls the men who are engaged in such arts not even human, and says that there is as great a difference between them and noble occupations, as there is between the convict's dishonored prison and the temple of the gods. Aristotle taught that the citizens of every well-regulated state should be free from servile labor (Politics, Bk. II. chap. 9). Again he says: "It follows that in the best governed states, where the citizens are really men of intrinsic and not relative goodness, none of them should be permitted to exercise any low mechanical employment or traffic, as being ignoble and destructive to virtue; neither should they who are destined for office be husbandmen; for leisure is necessary in order to improve in virtue, and to perform the duty which they owe the state" (Ibid. Bk. VII. chap. 9). In early Roman times the most noted men were not ashamed to handle the plow, and after the glories of war or the service of the state, they retired to their farms and spent their days in toil. But as the centuries passed, and wealth increased, and conquered nations were enslaved, labor became more and more dishonorable. The Feudal system has left us a bad inheritance, that work is ignoble and is unworthy the dignity of free men. To-day the impression more or less prevails that certain kinds of work are beneath man's dignity and are to be shunned or despised. The desire to escape manual toil is deeply ingrained in many minds, and is the source of many of the evils which afflict our modern society.

We all know that much of the work of this commonplace, matter-of-fact world is difficult and trying. Sancho Panza has said in suggestive phrase: "Fine words butter no parsnips." Fine words will not make work less work. To the great majority of our fellows life presents itself as a toilsome and severe struggle for existence. Only by hard labor can man wring his support out of an unwilling earth. Think for a moment of the conditions under which the work of this world is done; how so many of our fellows toil in mine and mill, in ditch and shop, on locomotive and street car, by dangerous engines and over poisonous vapors, in store and kitchen. Much of this toil seems hard and undignified and degrading. Does it? Then we have not learned the meaning of life and the divine significance of labor. If man's work in the world is commonplace, he may ennoble it by putting a fine and noble spirit into it. "I reckon two classes of idlers," says Charles Wagner, "those who are lazy, and those who grumble at their tasks." Let no man be ashamed of any honest work however hard or commonplace it may be. Let him remember that the Son of man was known as the Carpenter of Nazareth, and himself learned and followed a trade. I have heard men speak of the humiliation of Christ, as if toil was a part of it. Once and forever let us have done with this false and petty notion. A king is not one whit higher in the scale than a peasant ; nay, it may happen, as it often has, that the balance is entirely on the side of the peasant. The accessories and accidents of life, such as dress, occupation and social distinction have nothing to do with the moral worth of a man. The Son of man did the Father's will as truly at the carpenter's bench as in the sermon on the mount ; he manifested the Father's glory just as fully in the daily toil as in feeding the five thousand. He came to ennoble life, to reveal its divine significance, to show its true glory, to disclose the divineness of the commonplace. He chose his apostles from the ranks of toilers ; that glorious company of apostles could show men with the hard and horny hands of toil. The *Koran* tells how Gabriel, the bright archangel who stands before God, was sent to earth to do two things one day : One was to save King Solomon from the sin of forgetting the hour of prayer in pride over his royal treasures : the other was to help a little yellow ant on the side of Ararat which had grown tired, in getting food for its nest and was in danger of perishing in the rain. Some one has suggested that if two angels were sent of God to earth, one to preach an eloquent sermon in a great congregation, and the other to sweep a street-crossing, both would go with equal readiness and joy.

After all, what is work ? At bottom, all true work is a co-operation with God and has a divine significance. The artist takes a piece of rough stone and works and fashions it into an object of beauty, "a joy forever." The workman making shoes takes the shapeless pieces of leather and fashions them into objects of the greatest utility. Out of the formless they bring forth beauty and order. The shop-keeper weighing sugar is a link in the chain of providence between the eternal God and the hungry child. The farmer preparing his ground and planting his seed is only completing a process whose source is God. The farmer's harvest is no less God's harvest. The Father of men has worked hitherto and has prepared the means for man's effort. It is God who upholds the world by the word of his power; it is God who sends the sunlight streaming over hill and plain; it is God who gathers the clouds and sends the raindrops; it is God who makes the earth to bring forth flowers and give grain to the sower and bread to the eater. In all things, through all things, is God. If the farmer's work is commonplace, secular and degrading, God's work is likewise; if God's work is sacred, high and glorious, man's work is likewise. If it is a secular thing to plow a furrow and swing a sickle, it is secular work to make a seed grow and to create a stalk of corn.

Suppose we carry this process a step farther. The wheat is gathered and threshed, and is taken to the mill to be ground into flour. The miller does not create the force which runs his mill; he only co-operates with God, and belts his machinery on to the enginery of God. Thus he is another link in the chain of divine providence. But this flour is bought by the baker and by him made up into bread. The merchant again who retails this bread becomes another link in the great chain, and completes the process of feeding the hungry and keeping the world alive. At one end of the process is God; at the other end is man. Will any one pretend to say at just what link in the chain this process ceases to be sacred and glorious and becomes secular and degrading? All these workers —farmers, mechanics, millers, merchants—are so many agents and ministers of the divine bounty; from their hands men receive those useful and finished articles which have been produced by the co-operation of this great host of servants in God's vineyard. Well may Carlyle say: "Two men I honor and no third. First, the toil-worn craftsman that with earth-made implement laboriously conquers the earth, and makes her man's. . . . A second man I honor, and still more highly: him who is seen toiling for the spiritually indispensable; not only daily bread, but Bread of Life. . . . Unspeakably touching is it, however, when we find both dignities united; and he that toils outwardly for the lowest of man's wants is also toiling inwardly for the highest. Sublimer in this world know I nothing than a Peasant Saint, could such now anywhere be met with. Such a one will take thee back to Nazareth itself; thou wilt see the splendor of heaven spring forth from the humblest depths like a light shining in great darkness" (Sartor Resartus, Bk. III., ch. iv.).

What is true of the worker is no less true of the trader. Trade is an exchange of commodities or services, and being such it has a high moral significance. Trade and commerce are elemental facts of advancing human life. In a simple and primitive society the amount of trade between man and man and tribe and tribe is exceedingly small. But as life advances in the scale and wants multiply, trade becomes necessary. Nothing can be more evident than that the world is framed to be a place of trade. The diversity of aptitudes, of soil, climate, and productions necessitates trade between man and man and nation and nation. So long as one man has skill with tools and another skill with pen ; so long as one district produces coal and another produces wheat, that long trade will be necessary. It could easily be shown, did space permit, that commerce is one of the most potent forces making for the brotherhood of mankind and the civilization of the race. "Commerce," says Orville Dewey, "has always been an instrument in the hands of Providence for accomplishing nobler ends than promoting the wealth of nations. It has been the grand civilizer of nations. It has been the active principle in all civilization " (The Moral End of Business). The commercial nations have been the progressive nations. Civilization was born in the trading nations around the Mediterranean Sea. The trader is the shuttle carrying the woof on which the genius of history is weaving the race together in a great human brotherhood.

But we are not concerned here with this wider aspect of trade ; my purpose is to show that trade is a rendering of services, and as such has a moral significance. The trader or merchant who acts as the intermediary between the different workers of society, who brings the utilities of one section where they are produced to another section where they are needed, is most truly rendering great service to his fellows. In a complex society a division of labor is necessary ; and the merchant as truly renders service as the man who produces commodities.

Two things are made evident by all this. First, a man's daily calling is his priestly service to God and man. One truth has been emphasized in these chapters from first to last : the division of life into the sacred and the secular is false, mischievous and unchristian. A man's work in the world, whatever it may be, provided it is honest and proper work, is his divine calling. How often we have heard business men lament that business made such demands upon their time and energy that little or no opportunity remained for the service of God. How common also it has been for men to speak of making some money and then retiring from business and devoting themselves more fully to Christian work. There is a most subtle error lurking at the heart of all such thoughts. Business rightly done is a service of God in the welfare of man. The man's business is his altar of service and sacrifice. Any position in life, any work given man, affords a standing ground from which to reach forth and serve mankind. A man's work, whatever it is, is the sphere of his religion's manifestation, and that work is a divine calling. All labor, all trades, all business, have ends beyond themselves. Devoutness is not a matter of place but of spirit. Not the kind of work done is well pleasing to God, but the spirit shining through it. The merchant who makes his counter an altar of sacrifice is most truly serving his day and generation according to the will of God. He pays his employés the best wages possible ; he takes an interest in their welfare ; he studies the needs of society and brings commodities from afar to satisfy those needs ; he sells the best goods for the money and thus truly serves his customers. Every transaction in that store bears the sign of the cross. Wise work, Ruskin tells us, is work done with God : foolish work is work against God. The Kingdom of God is wide-reaching, all-embracing. There is not a spindle turning in any mill, there is not a locomotive drawing its heavy freight, not a plow turning a furrow, not a merchant weighing flour, not a housewife sweeping a room, that may not have a place within the kingdom and work to the glory of God in the service of man. Every man who, in an honest and good heart is working for cleaner literature and better laws, for better skill in trade and larger service in commerce, is a worker in the great Kingdom of God. When men see that they may work in behalf of the kingdom by the way they run their factories, make laws, edit newspapers, pay wages, mine coal, plow fields, a great change will come over the life and thought of the world. The mechanic may be as necessary to the coming of the Kingdom of God as the preacher; and the merchant may yet play as important a place as the missionary.

And secondly, the way in which one fulfills his daily tasks at once makes and reveals his character. Faithfulness, energy, honesty can be shown in the most trifling things. Work means character. The work is the man come to manifestation. In the last analysis it will appear that this world is designed as a training-place for character. The very hardness and difficulty of man's lot call out his hidden capabilities; they develop energy and fidelity; the very hardness puts iron into his blood, fire into his eye and persistence into his will; perseverance, patience, fidelity become the crowning virtues. What are the qualities which enter into the making of right character? Are they not these very virtues of energy, patience, perseverance, faithfulness, love and sacrifice? And where can these qualities be so fully gained or so truly shown as in the common occupations and tasks of daily life? "He that is faithful in a very little is faithful also in much: and he that is unrighteous in a very little is unrighteous also in much." "Man's character has been moulded by his every-day work, and by the material resources which he thereby procures, more than by any other influence, unless it be that of his religious ideals : and the two great forming agencies of the world's history have been the religious and the economic. . . . For the business by which a person earns his livelihood generally fills his thoughts during by far the greater part of those hours in which his mind is at its best ; during them his character is being formed by the way in which he uses his faculties in his work, by the thoughts and the feelings which it suggests, and by the relations to his associates in work, his employers, or his employés " (Marshall : Principles of Economics, p. 1).

II. THE MORAL PRINCIPLES FOR THE MILL AND MARKET.

Carlyle used to speak of the science of Economics, as "that dismal science." Much of the teaching that passed current in his day as Economic Science deserved that reproachful term. For that teaching was almost wholly devoid of moral content, and made wealth an end in itself instead of a means to an end. Selfishness it was taught was the basis of economic activity ; each man was expected to look out for just one person in a trade —himself. Men were expected to be kind and unselfish in other relations of life, but not in trade and business. A recent writer so far perpetuates this error as to say : "Economics can never be rightly invaded by ethics ; its undeniable province is the facts and laws of human nature that concern the pursuit and expenditure of wealth. We have no choice about the intellectual acceptance of these truths" (Gilman: Socialism and the American Spirit, p. 250). In much of the thought of the past generations it has been assumed that the various sciences were separate and distinct spheres of life, with no intercourse allowable between these alien worlds. Than this no conception can be more erroneous, more mischievous. Ethical principles cannot work in a vacuum: their undeniable sphere of manifestation is human life with its interests, relations and activities. Often has it been said that charity is one thing and business is another; that religion and trade have nothing to do with one another. A vigorous and careful writer has said that the one who should prosecute his search thoughtfully and fearlessly, intent only upon the truth, must at length find that the "whole farrago which has so long passed for political economy is true only of irrational animals and is altogether inapplicable to rational man" (Ward: Psychic Factors of Civilization, p. 279). Much of what has passed for economic science would have seemed antiquated and Egyptian to Moses; and Socrates would have been stoned on the streets of Athens as a corrupter of the youth, for teaching some things that have been said under the name of "economic science."

Fortunately a new science of economics is being created in which ethical considerations hold a first place. Wealth is no longer seen to be an end in itself; wealth is weal, human weal. "Wealth consists of the relative-weal-constituting elements in man's material environment" (Clark : The Philosophy of Wealth, p. 4). "Communion through the material world with God is expressed by the word property," says Brownson. But more than this the Christian principle assumes that every part of life is subject to the dominion of Jesus Christ. The Kingdom of God is all-inclusive and comprehends every interest and relation and activity of man. The Christian principle implies that the Christ spirit and the Christ life are the law of life in trade no less than in the family and in the church. The law of Christ bids us love our fellows, not alone in mission contributions, but in bargains and sales. The law of Christ imposes the obligation to bear one another's burdens, not only in the church but in the market. To believe in the Lord is to take his precepts down into the mill and the store, into the shop and the countingroom, and stand or fall with them there. The Bible is as much in place in the countingroom as on the church pulpit; its precepts are as binding upon the factory as upon the church. To be a Christian disciple is to make the spirit of Christ's life the law of one's life. To believe in the Golden Rule is to refuse to engage in any transaction which is not mutually advantageous to both parties. The strong are to bear the infirmities of the weak and not to please themselves, as much in the railroad company as in the prayer meeting.

The acceptance of this principle as the law of life in mill and market is the first requirement. The application of this principle must be left more or less to the personal conscience. No rules are here attempted, as no rules can be given which will apply in all circumstances. Besides, the application of great principles gives opportunity for the weighing of motives, the forecasting of results, the choice of alternatives. The principle is that we are to love our neighbors, to bear their burdens, to seek their interests in doing work, in paying wages, in selling commodities; that we are to please our brother unto edification in the stock exchange and in the corporation. This principle is absolute in its requirement and universal in its sweep, and can admit no abatement under any circumstances. Not one of us may measure up to this perfect law of God; but we are justified by faith when we have a vision of God's righteousness and make choice of his will. A few illustrations of these general principles may be suggestive.

1. Every man should be willing to earn all he receives.

He should be willing to toil by sweat of brow or sweat of brain for all that comes into his hands. There is an ominous tendency in modern times, growing out of the consuming haste to be rich, to escape toil by various makeshifts, by speculation, by exploiting the labor of others. As an illustration of this passion for a fortune without any moral sense of its meaning and responsibility, Mayor S. M. Jones, of Toledo, said in the presence of a little group of friends that he had put this question to probably fifty American millionaires: " Why do you want to be rich ? " Not one had given him an answer that was in the least satisfactory. One man's answer was : " Why does a man want anything ? I want to be rich because I like it." Getting on in the world has almost come to mean getting rich. And Scripture long ago declared : "He that maketh haste to be rich shall not be innocent." Men are not content to labor faithfully, receiving what comes to them in the appointment of providence ; they are in haste to be rich ; and to reach this end they must resort too often to questionable means. There is a speculation that is just and fair, a speculation advantageous to the community. But there is also a speculation which passes beyond the safety line and becomes a subtle form of dishonesty and exploitation. To attempt to discuss and define just speculation and discriminate it from gambling speculation would carry us too far into the region of casuistry. "What, then, is gambling speculation ? It is buying or selling without the power or the disposition to bring about any transfer of real goods at all ; it is selling what you do not own, or buying what you do not expect or wish to acquire ; it is going through the form of purchase and sale without any thought of actual goods or actual trade ; it is just betting on the future prices of things" (Andrews: Wealth and Moral Law, p. 72). Again: "I say therefore, that business gambling, sham speculation, nominal trading which leaves actual values out of view, differs in no moral particular from gaming at faro, roulette, or bluff. It contributes to a popular gambling mania which causes infinite loss, poverty, and misery; he who engages in it toys with the stability of his character in its most delicate parts; and further, so far as he gains livelihood or fortune from this source, as many do, his gain is theft, being at the expense of his fellow-men, a taking from society with no return" (Ibid., pp. 74, 75). In fullest truth it may be said that some of the speculative methods and stock-jobbing operations of our day are nothing more nor less than polite and respectable ways of violating the Eighth Commandment. "To start a company and to induce people to take shares in it by false representations of the amount of the subscribed capital and of its probable success is to steal" (Dale: The Ten Commandments, p. 197). Ruskin has shown that the real source of great riches consists in obtaining so much victory over your neighbor as "to obtain the direction of his work, and to take the profits of it. No man can become largely rich by his personal toil. The work of his own hands, wisely directed, will always maintain himself and his family, and make fitting provision for his age. But it is only by the discovery of some method of taxing the labor of others that he can become opulent" (Munera Pulveris, sec. 139). It is possible that there is some slight exaggeration in this; it does not allow for the wealth that may be won through some fortunate and useful invention; but in the main Ruskin is right. The Emperor of China has said: "If there was a man who did not work or a woman that was idle, somebody must suffer cold and hunger in the empire." The principle, however, is clear: Every man should be willing to earn by his own toil whatever comes into his hands, and not seek to charm it out of the hand of his neighbor.

2. The application of this principle obliges each to regard the other as his brother, and to render him the largest and highest possible service. This applies to all classes and conditions of men, to workingmen and merchants, to employers, to traders, to farmers. Suppose the workingmen of a certain line of manufacture could so combine as to control all the skilled workmen in that line of industry. For them to meet and demand certain wage of their employees without respect to their interests or the state of trade would be a violation of the law of love. On the other hand, suppose that the manufacturers of a certain line of goods should effect a combination and agree to pay so much wages to their employés without respect to their interests or claims; no less must we pronounce this transaction essentially unjust and unchristian. It is by the harmonious combination of laborer and employer that satisfactory results

are secured. When either party, because of its possession of strength, takes advantage of the other party, injustice is done, and the law of love is violated. "The matching of strength against weakness is contrary to fighting codes; equal armor and equal weapons were the rule of knighthood" (Clark: The Philosophy of Wealth, p. 165). Again: "A few men without employment and a few employers without souls are the conditions of a general reduction of wages below the point to which more legitimate causes would reduce them" (Ibid., p. 169).

The royal law of Christ expects the workingman to give the largest and best service to his employer, and to seek his interests,—in a word, to render the largest possible service. On the other hand, that law obliges the employer to treat his employés as brothers and to pay them the largest wages that the state of market will allow. Employers and employed are partners in trade; they are brother men, and each must look not only on the things of self, but each also on the things of others. The success of the business depends quite as much upon the interest and fidelity of employés as upon the skill and management of employers. Of course superior skill will always command superior wages; to equalize wages is to put a premium upon mediocrity. Laborer and capitalist both take risks and jeopardize much; the capitalist may jeopardize the luxuries of his home and his capital; the workingman often jeopardizes his very life and the welfare of his family. The relation between employer and employed is more than a cash nexus; the parties in every transaction are not aliens, not machines, but brother men, and are to be mutually cherished as brothers. It is not too much to expect that under the influence of the Christian principle there will arise a class of "Captains of Industry" who will seek to organize industries with other aims than selfish accumulation, and will attack the problems of society in the spirit of the Golden Rule.

3. This principle forbids one to take any undue advantage of his fellows. The fundamental idea of trade and commerce is a rendering of services or an exchange of commodities. The implication is that this exchange is mutually advantageous to both parties. The old idea that the parties in the business transaction are enemies, and any advantage may be taken the one of the other, belongs to the primitive, military, and jungle plane of society. The Christian conception of humanity obliges us to regard men not as enemies to be beaten but as brothers to be served. Hence all commerce between men is but an exchange between friends, and each desires that it be wholly just as between members of the same family. The best illustration of our principle is a case stated by Cicero in *De Officiis*.

A merchant of Alexandria arrived in Rhodes in a time of famine with a cargo of grain. He knew that a fleet of vessels loaded with similar grain was on its way from Alexandria, and would soon arrive in the same harbor. Cicero raises the question whether this grain merchant shall conceal this information from the Rhodians, and, taking advantage of their ignorance and necessity, demand the highest famine price for his grain. And this old teacher of morals decides that he was bound in conscience to inform the Rhodians of the facts in the case. For any bargain or contract implies fair-dealing and truth-telling. The man who fixes the price of an article is supposed to do so in good faith, basing his price upon his knowledge of the goods and all the circumstances in the case. Suppose that this grain merchant had taken advantage of the people's necessity and had concealed the information in his possession; his price for the grain would not be fixed in good faith and he would be guilty of falsehood. But had he fixed a price based upon his opinion of probability as to when the other vessels would arrive, his transaction would be fair. The fundamental fact in a right bargain, we repeat, is mutual advantage. Of course, to the one who assumes that neither party is expected to act in good faith, this interpretation of the case in hand will be unsatisfactory. But we have assumed, and we shall assume, that the man who fixes a price bases that price upon his judgment of the goods, the information in his possession, and the mutual advantage of all parties.*

* For a full discussion of this question of Cicero, see Orville Dewey's Works, and also "Capital and Labor," a prize book.

Not selfishness, but love is the basis of all right economic science. The purely selfish, competitive instinct rules in the jungle across tribal lines; tigers and lions know no altruism, no love. But Professor Drummond has shown that among animals of the same species, at least, there is the beginning of altruism, a struggle for the life of others. Competition, it has been assumed, will settle all things; the law of supply and demand is inexorable; each man must look out for himself. But competition is sometimes most cruel and may be wholly unjust. "Competition without moral restraints is a monster as completely antiquated as the saurians of which the geologists tell us" (Clark: The Philosophy of Wealth, p. 151). All students of economic affairs know "that prices of most of the staple commodities consumed by mankind have no necessary relation to the cost of producing them and placing them in the hands of the consumer" (Ward: Psychic Factors of Civilization, p. 327). This same writer also shows that competition not only involves great waste, but it prevents the maximum development. He makes clear that society will attain its maximum development and waste will be reduced by the larger sway of other factors. Too long it has been assumed that men are free to do their brothers to the death, provided only, "the instrument be a bargain and the arena a market." Too long also this conception of trade has justified the lines:

Our life is like a narrow raft,
Afloat upon the hungry sea,
Whereon is but a little space ;
And each man, eager for a place,
Doth thrust his brother in the sea,
And so the sea is salt with tears,
And so our life is worn with fears.

The resolute determination to live and trade on the moral and loving basis will require strong faith and fine courage. This life-long allegiance to the Christian principle, which sometimes means loss, will try the temper of any man's spirit. The strength, the coherence, the fiber of his character will be tested here as nowhere else in the world. "I think we all find it the hardest and most hopeless work of all our lives," said Phillips Brooks, "the effort to keep our highest ideas and our commonest occupations in constant and healthy contact with each other" (Influence of Jesus, p. 21). But the degree in which one does this measures most accurately the fineness and fiber of his character.

Nothing can be more important than the enthronement of the Christian spirit as the law of life in the industrial world. So far as men learn to do this, they will learn to regard their daily work as a divine calling and a priestly sacrifice. In every relation of man with man there is a field for justice. And Aristotle has suggested that wherever there is a field for justice there is also a field for love. And Fremantle has supplemented this by saying that wherever there is a field for love there is also a field for the operation of the divine Spirit. In one of the European cities there is a temple through which is a passage-way into a market. Those who pass into the market to buy and sell may turn aside to kneel at the altar of prayer and to commune with God.

Scientific writers have maintained that struggle is necessary to the full development of life. This we can readily believe : life means effort ; the way to victory lies across a battlefield ; character is an achievement. But it is easily conceivable that all the discipline of struggle necessary to any man can come through the struggle for the life of others. Surely it is not too much to expect that increasing numbers of Captains of Industry will arise who will organize industries for the benefit of all mankind. Under the increasing sway of the Christian spirit, "we may look forward to a time when the unselfish motives will have fuller development, when the wish to benefit the community will stimulate men's energies more fully than competition, and when the public recognition of service, and the gratitude of those who are benefited, may be an adequate guarantee for efficiency" (Fremantle : The World as the Subject of Redemption, p. 348). At any rate it holds true now that all work honestly done receives its due reward in the character of the doer ; it is a co-operation with God in the creation of order and beauty ; all trade that fulfills the royal law becomes a divine service and contributes unto the building up of the body of society in love. Thus is fulfilled the old motto framed by the monks, *Laborare est orare.*

CHAPTER X.

THE CITIZEN AND HIS POLITICS.

And I John saw the holy city, New Jerusalem, coming down from God out of heaven, prepared as a bride adorned for her husband. And there shall in no wise enter into it anything unclean, or he that maketh an abomination and a lie.—*The Apocalypse.*

Yes, the vision of the Apocalypse is for us also. Beyond these crowded thoroughfares which bewilder us, these crushing palaces of commerce which overwhelm us, this sordid glare which dazzles and saddens us, rises before the believer the holy city, pure and still.—BROOKE FOSS WESTCOTT.

From history we learn that the great function of religion has been the founding and sustaining of states.—J. R. SEELEY.

Government is not transient, nor a necessary evil, but eternal in the heart of God, and is the discipline and education of the people in the image and right of the only perfectly governed man the world has known, the man Christ Jesus.— GEORGE D. HERRON.

THERE are three institutions known to man which are divine in origin, the family, the church, and the state. Each of these has its own functions, though covering much the same sphere. Each has its own mission, though they all work toward the one common end. Each is a medium through which man ascends to God, and through each the life of God is getting itself reborn into the life of humanity. Each is an outlying principality of that kingdom which is over all. Each aims to realize the ideals of the kingdom of God, to translate them into human lives, and fulfill them in human relations. As the sunlight which fills the heavens and floods the earth seeks to get itself reborn and translated into the wheatfield and the rose ; so the life and righteousness and love of the kingdom seek to get themselves incarnated in human lives, manifested in human relations, and fixed in human institutions.

" Life cannot be completed within the sheltered precincts of the home. As the years go on the child enters naturally into a wider sphere. The friendships of school, the intercourse of business, reveal to the growing boy new obligations, new joys, new temptations, new conflicts through which the lessons of earlier discipline are extended and applied. He learns to be one of many, and in a varied companionship to give definiteness to that which he has in common with his fellows. In this way the idea of the nation, the society of neighbors, is called into active exercise to supplement the idea of the family, the society of kinsmen in blood. At the same time the life of the family is seen in its continuity and in its breadth in the life of the nation. Thus the nation is found to be the second type, the second broadening circle of social life " (Westcott : Social Aspects of Christianity, pp. 35, 36). No man has attained unto the measure of the stature of Christian character, till he has learned to honor and fulfill all the relationships which he sustains to his fellows. The great virtues of Christianity are largely social virtues, that is, they are virtues which have their subsistence in the relation of man with man. It is in the wide sphere of the state that the virtues of love and forbearance, fidelity and humility, patience and goodness have their full meaning and come to their perfect work. At this stage of our study it is fitting that we consider the Christian Citizen as a member of the social order, seeking to realize the deeper meaning of the state, and endeavoring to fulfill every social and political duty to the glory of God.

I. The Divine Meaning of the State.

The state is involved in the very constitution of man. Aristotle long ago taught that man is by nature a political being; the man who is naturally, not accidentally, unfit for society is either inferior or superior to man. We are all dependent upon one another, and the state is at once a confession of our personal incompleteness, and is the divine provision for meeting this lack. Man is made for fellowship, and cannot attain unto perfection and fullness of being in isolation and solitude. Thought cannot conceive of a single, isolated, unrelated individual. Each man's life is linked in with other lives by ties which cannot be evaded or escaped. Our lives touch other lives, and the state is the provision which God has made for the right adjustment of these human relationships. Apart from human fellowship man cannot come to his best estate, as the rose cannot bloom without soil and sunshine and rain. Our personal life is rooted in the life of humanity; it flourishes in that soil, and draws its richest nourishment, and unfolds its highest possibilities in that soil. Shakespeare, raised from infancy among apes, would be a speechless, unthinking brute. Without attempting to go into detail it may not be unnecessary to consider briefly the place which the state holds in the economy of life.

The state is the organ of the political consciousness in man. Man comes into the world endowed with the instinct which impels him to seek association with his kind. Each man is a member of an order or life which reaches before him and after him: no one can stand alone, absolute, independent. Man, by the very constitution of his being, is a creature of relationships, and it is only in and through these relationships that he comes to maturity, perfection and self-consciousness. Various views have been advanced as to the origin of states; these views we shall not stop to notice. It matters not what theory of the origin of states be adopted, one fact remains: each man finds in himself an impulse and consciousness of which the state becomes the realization and expression. In the persons who compose the state there was an implicit and subjective consciousness of oneness, and this consciousness becomes explicit and objective in the state. The ties that bind men together are ties which they did not invent and which they cannot destroy.

The state is the institute of right relations. The origin of the state is to be found in the nature of man. "A state," as Plato makes Socrates say, "arises as I conceive out of the needs of mankind; no one is self-sufficient, but all of us have many wants. Can any other origin of a state be imagined?" "None," replied Adeimantus (Republic, Bk. II.). A very simple condition of human life may not need a state. Robinson Crusoe alone with Man Friday can get along very well without government. But the moment Crusoe returns to civilized and social life, which he was so willing to do, that moment the relations of life multiply and the state becomes necessary to correlate and adjust these relations. The state we may say is a co-ordinating apparatus; it endeavors to apprehend the rights which belong to human nature and to co-ordinate and conserve these rights. The state finds men existing in certain relations with one another; it endeavors to ascertain what are the relations which should subsist between them; it defines these relations and puts upon them the stamp of its approval and makes them obligatory. The state does not create the relations of father and son, of husband and wife, of neighbor and neighbor, of man and property. But the state with its authority guards and sanctions these relations and puts the stamp of obligation upon them. The state thus becomes the institute of right relations; it becomes the guarantee to each man that his rights shall be respected and the proper order of the community shall be maintained. The laws of the state become pledges of security, agreements of fair dealing, rules of social conduct, laws which each is under obligation to observe in his dealings with his neighbors. In a simple form of society the relationships of man with man are few; and hence the rights defined are few. But as society becomes more complex these relationships multiply, men are driven closer together, they become more dependent upon one another; now the relationships of life which press so closely upon all become intolerable, unless they are right relations.

The state is also a partnership of men in all good. From various sides the state has been attacked and its usefulness denied. It has been maintained that the state is an unnecessary evil, and hence is unworthy the support of all right-thinking men. Possibly the most prominent and pronounced advocate of this view is the great Russian, Count Leo Tolstoi. It can easily be shown that Tolstoi is not consistent with himself. His words however are worthy of careful consideration, because he has called attention to some of the great and serious abuses of government. Again: others have maintained that government is an evil, but for the present is a necessary evil. The advocates of this theory maintain that the state is necessary in an evolving and imperfect society, but that it, being evil, must soon or late disappear. Over against these views we set these noble words of Burke: "Without civil society man could not by any possibility arrive at the perfection of which his nature is capable, nor even make a remote and faint approach to it. . . . He who gave our nature to be perfected by our virtue, willed also the necessary means to its perfection. —He willed therefore the state—he willed its connection with the source and original archetype of all perfection" (Reflections on the Revolution in France, 370, Bohn). Men are not equal in endowment, in talent, in power. For a long time to come the strong will be under obligation to bear the infirmities of the weak. The state is the medium through which the power of one becomes the good of all. Individual effort may do much for the improvement of other individuals; but individual effort to be highly successful must be supported by the social order: it must work through the social order. The state is in the best sense the medium through which personal power is conveyed to all and is made effective for all. The state is the only organ or medium great enough to express these varied powers of men, the only medium through which men can most effectually co-operate in the attainment of social perfection. Political visionaries have drawn beautiful pictures of the blessedness and freedom of man in what they are pleased to call a state of nature. But no such men have been found; such men are not perfect men in the full meaning of the term.

Worthy of all acceptance are the words of Burke, one of the clearest political thinkers of the world: "The state ought not to be considered as nothing better than a partnership agreement in a trade of pepper and coffee, calico or tobacco, or some other such low concern, to be taken up for a little temporary interest, and to be dissolved by the fancy of the parties. It is to be looked on with reverence; because it is not a partnership in things subservient only to the gross animal existence of a temporary and perishable nature. It is a partnership in all science; a partnership in all art; a partnership in every virtue and in all perfection" (French Revolution, p. 368).

The state is an instrument through which God declares and exercises his authority over men. Government is a usurpation to be resisted and changed, if it is not a divine ordinance, deriving authority from him who is Lord of all, existing for the one purpose of fulfilling his ends. God's right to rule over men in all relations is a right which he has never surrendered, and which he will never surrender to any earthly government. Back of the state is God: back of the civil statute is the righteousness of God; back of the earthly ruler is the King of kings. The Biblical teaching on this subject is plain and unmistakable. The underlying idea of the Judaic legislation was the kingship of Jehovah. Judges, rulers, and kings were not regarded as sources of authority, but only as channels. The judges are charged to judge righteously: "For the judgment is God's." Back of the king was Jehovah, the supreme Ruler whose will was the standard of the national conscience, and all kingly and temporal authority is derived from him. To this standard the conscience of the nation ever must appeal, and by it all cases are to be tested. The demand of the people for a king who should be a visible source of authority was regarded by Jehovah as an act of national apostasy: "They have not rejected thee, but they have rejected me, that I should not be king over them" (R. V., 1 Samuel viii. 7).

The New Testament teaching does not set aside nor destroy this old conception; rather it enlarges and fulfills it. Paul says: "There is no power but of God; the powers that be are ordained of God." He bids Christians pray for rulers, and for all who are in authority; the ruler is the minister, the deacon of God to thee for good. In the life of the Lord Jesus we have one striking illustration of his conception of the meaning of human government. The reference though indirect is all the more significant, When on trial before Pilate he is questioned, "Whence art thou?" The question contains a hint that there is some mysterious power lying back of this strange prisoner. Pilate becomes irritated at the refusal of Jesus to answer his questions of curiosity, and says: "Speakest thou not unto me? Knowest thou not that I have power to crucify thee, and have power to release thee?" The Roman Governor thinks of this power as something that he can use as caprice may dictate. The answer of Jesus is most significant, and is one of the most suggestive words he ever spoke: "Thou couldest have no power at all against me, except it were given thee from above." The words imply that Pilate's power, which he regards as arbitrary and irresponsible, power which he is about to misuse so flagrantly, has its source in that mysterious unseen world whence the Son of man has come. This power, which Pilate thinks himself free to use as he pleases, is power delegated to him from the unseen world. They contain also a gentle but searching appeal intended to remind the Roman that he also is accountable to the Judge and King of all the earth. Pilate was a Roman politician, and had probably obtained this appointment through intrigue or influence; for this reason he was hardly expected to recognize the high and divine meaning of the position which he occupied. But the Jewish Sanhedrin understood well the great truth that all human earthly rulers were the representatives of God, and were appointed to execute the judgments of God. That government was a divine ordinance was one of the fundamental ideas of the Jewish nation. For the Sanhedrin to misuse this divine ordinance, and make it the instrument of their evil designs, was one of the greatest and most heinous sins. On this account they who delivered Jesus to the Roman Governor, and demanded that he prostitute his high office in carrying out their wicked devices, were guilty of the blackest crime. Government, which was a divine ordinance, and should be used to divine ends, they desecrated and prostituted, when they made it the instrument of caprice and self-will. From all this it is plain that the state is an ordinance of God, government is his instrument for the protection of man, the avenging of wrong, and the establishment of righteousness.

II. THE CITIZENSHIP OF THE CHRISTIAN DISCIPLE.

No institution, no power on earth, so holds in its grasp the weal or woe of the millions now living and of the millions yet to come as the state. The social order, the national sentiments, the governmental regulations, influence immeasurably every soul that comes within their reach. More and more men are coming to see that the state has a moral end, and that the real work of citizens consists in so shaping institutions and so framing legislation that conditions may be secured favorable to the development of noble characters. The true wealth of states is to be measured, not in terms of material resources, but in the growth of moral personality. Says Aristotle: "A state exists for the sake of a good life, and not for the sake of life only; if life only were the object, slaves and brute animals might form a state; but they cannot, for they have no share in happiness or in a life of free choice. Whence it may be inferred that virtue must be the serious care of a state which truly deserves the name : for, without this ethical end, the community becomes a mere alliance which differs only in place from alliances of which the members live apart ; and law is only a convention, a 'surety to one another of justice,' as the sophist Lycophron says, and has no real power to make the citizens good" (Politics, Bk. III. 9). The state is the nursery of men, and unless noble men are being produced, every great end of the state's existence is thwarted. Politics is the science of social welfare, and has at heart the achievement of a social order in which the ideals of humanity shall be realized.

Since this is so, every citizen should be a politician in the larger and better sense of the word. This means that every member of the state should be concerned in all that makes for the welfare of the state. That noble word " politics " needs to be redeemed from the mire and the gutter, through which it has been dragged by groundling partisans. It is said that Dwight L. Moody, in conversation with a noted evangelist, a short time before an important election, inquired : "What is the political outlook?" "I don't know anything about it," was the answer. "My citizenship is in heaven." "Better get it down to earth for the next sixty days," was the reply of the wise man. To play the shirk in one's political duty is as serious and as sinful as to play the shirk in the home or in the church. Nay, it is often more serious, as the interests involved in the state are often larger and more urgent than the interests of the church or the home.

In the providence of God it has come about that the citizens of the kingdom of God in nearly all nations are directly or indirectly the makers and administrators of law. There are many questions growing out of this fact, upon which the New Testament throws no direct light. Christianity is committed to no particular form of government, whether monarchy or democracy. But the principles of the kingdom are to be the informing, vitalizing principles of each and every nation. The idea of the kingdom of God supplies us with civil and social ideals, with constructive and regulative principles the highest and noblest. The essential truths of Christianity are architectonic, and furnish at once the foundation basis, and the regulative ideal for the social order. Soon or late, the Christian disciple must face these alternatives: whether he will have nothing to do with social and political affairs; or whether he will claim every political privilege and make his civil and social privileges the flowering and fruitage of the Christian spirit. He must do one or the other. Either he must refrain from all participation in civil affairs; or he must make his civil acts the expression of his Christian convictions. To refrain from all participation in civil affairs does not commend itself to the better Christian conscience as the wise course. The race has not progressed backwards, and all progress towards popular government has not been a retrogression. Whether all men are willing to accept the responsibilities of citizenship is one question; the fact remains that in many nations to-day they are charged with these responsibilities, and cannot evade or escape them without being recreant to high trusts. A great and significant movement is going on in the world to-day, a movement fraught with immeasurable woe or immeasurable blessing to countless numbers of our race. The great nations of the world are launching forth full on the tide of popular government. Slowly the scepter of authority has passed from the monarch to the few, and from the few to the many. To-day, in half-a-dozen leading nations, the people are practically supreme, and more or less determine the laws and manage the government. This means that all the people are summoned to participate in the responsibilities of the social welfare. At a great price humanity has gained this privilege. The past three centuries have witnessed a great change; the transit and transfer of power first from the monarch to the aristocracy; then from the aristocracy to the people. Beyond the king there were always the nobles to act as a last resort, and conserve the prerogatives of authority and the power of the laws. Now, however, the political power and the throne of authority have been lodged with the people themselves, and the last reserves are called into the field. In a popular government the responsibility of the state is laid upon the minds and consciences of the people. They must face all the problems of the state; they must consider the social welfare; they must frame legislation, they must form the nation's conscience; in a word, every citizen is called to bear the burden and heat of the struggle for life and progress in the state.

1. The Christian citizen takes an interest in everything that concerns the welfare and progress of the state. This means that first of all he is a patriot. Much of what passes for patriotism is utterly unworthy that high name. Pride in one's country with many passes for patriotism, but it is not. Dislike of a foreign power with many is interpreted as patriotism, but it is not. Strong attachment to one's political party with a large class passes for real patriotism, but partisanship is not patriotism. It is all too common for the partisan to construe the welfare of the nation in terms of the party's platform. Instead of this they should construe their party in terms of the nation's interests. Patriotism is that deep, strong passion for the higher, larger interests of the people. Finely has the poet sung :

> " Breathes there a man with soul so dead,
>   Who never to himself hath said,
>   This is my own, my native land,
>   Whose heart hath ne'er within him burned,
>   As home his footsteps he hath turned,
>   From wandering on a foreign strand ? "

The highest life that ever walked this earth was intensely patriotic. It is true that he came as the Saviour of men and his mission was to all the world; but he felt the spell of his native hills: he loved the history of his people and shared in the glories of the past. The bards of the nation sang of Jerusalem "beautiful for situation." "If I forget thee, O Jerusalem, let my right hand forget her cunning." Most pathetic is the Master's lament over the city of his love: "O Jerusalem, Jerusalem, how often would I have gathered thy children together, even as a hen gathereth her chickens under her wings, and ye would not." We know also of his great disciple Paul, how he cried: "I could wish that myself were accursed from Christ for my brethren, my kinsmen according to the flesh." Patriotism is this deep, strong passion of the soul in behalf of the higher interests of the citizens. Our sympathies are to be as broad as the world, and our parish is to be all mankind: but we can best fulfill our worldwide mission by making our own nation all that it ought to be and all that it may be. To know the past of one's nation; to enter into the present need; to live and work for her future; this is patriotism.

2. The Christian citizen will govern his civil duty by moral principles. This is one of the things that should go without saying; but alas, it does not. Moral principles have been more or less applied to the personal and family life of men; we have come to expect men to be pure in life, unselfish in the home, self-sacrificing and without guile. But

somehow, men have been very slow and very reluctant to apply moral principles to their public duties. Men, who would be shocked at the thought of a lie in the home or duplicity in the church, will deceive in politics and practice all sorts of guile. Christianity teaches, if it teaches anything, that for all our acts we are to give an account to God. It teaches also that the will of God is universal in its sweep and absolute in its requirements, a law for men, for homes, for churches, for political parties, for halls of legislation. God will bring every work into judgment, whether in the home or in the state. We must all give an account for our political deeds and misdeeds, as fully as for our personal and family affairs. This is a truth so simple and elementary that one is almost ashamed to speak of it. But simple as it is, many men, many otherwise good men, practically deny it in conduct. On all sides this truth of the accountability to God for our political doings is practically denied and evaded. The man in office is made to feel that he is answerable to the party machine through whose agency he has won office. Public office is a public trust, for which the holder must give an account to God. In practical affairs, however, public office is regarded as a party gift, to be used for the interests and advantages of the party. The man who acts on this dictum is a traitor to his trust; he is selling his soul for a mess of party pottage; he is recreant to every high trust of God or man. A brilliant United States senator recently said : "The decalogue and the sermon on the mount have nothing to do with a political campaign." He explained himself afterwards to the effect that he was describing things as they are and not as they ought to be. Certainly the man who believes in God must set his face like flint against any such methods. In the family and in the church it is assumed that a man will leave his own personal interests out of the account, and will act with a supreme consideration for the welfare of others; he will live in these spheres as one who must give account. But in public affairs it is quietly assumed that the man in office will make the most of that office for himself and for his party. It has come to this in many communities, that a man is hardly expected to be interested in the affairs of his city or state unless he has some office to seek or some interest to subserve.

A man's duty in the state is just as sacred and obligatory as his duty in the family or in the church. Whatever one does in word or in deed is to be done in the name of the Lord Jesus. The Christian citizen who prays : "Father in heaven : thy will be done on earth, as in heaven," is so to speak, so to live, so to vote, that his life and word and ballot may hasten on that glad day. All men would say that it is a prostitution of the office of minister for a bad man to stand in a Christian pulpit, and to make that office a means of selfish gratification. The world has come to insist upon this : that the men who stand in Christian pulpits shall be above reproach, men who love the truth, men who hate covetousness, men who fear God and seek righteousness. But it is just as wrong, just as unfit, just as degrading, to the idea of government for a bad, selfish, untruthful, dishonest man to hold office in the state. There is one law, only one, for every man, for every part of life, for every institution on earth—the holy will of the eternal God. And men are no more free to play the knave and the cheat in the legislature than in the family or in the church.

3. The Christian citizen will do all in his power to secure the enactment of good laws, and to bring in a better social order. One great purpose of all law is to declare what is socially right and wrong. What law allows as a rule the conscience of man approves, and what law condemns the conscience of the people does not commend. One great function of law is to be the standard of social judgment and conduct. The legislation of a nation is at once the expression of the nation's life and the determiner of the nation's morality. "Good laws elevate men; bad laws, if persisted in for a series of years, will degrade any society. It is one of the greatest blessings to live under wise laws administered by an upright government, and obeyed and carried out by good and stanch citizens; it is most grateful and animating to a generous heart, and a mind which cheerfully assists in the promotion of the general good, or salutary institutions" (Francis Lieber: Political Ethics).

More important even than the written statute is the regard for right and truth which lies back of the statute. Deeper than all questions of expediency is the great question of what is morally right. It must ever be remembered that right and wrong are not determined by the mob at the foot of Sinai, but by the will of him who dwells in the mount. Right and wrong, it cannot be too strongly emphasized, are not the creations of the ballot-box; justice and injustice are not the will of the majority. To read that law whose dwelling-place is none other than the bosom of the living God is the business of the human law maker. The real law maker endeavors to express and realize in human legislation the moral distinctions which are wrought into the very fabric of the universe. The only argument adducible in favor of any law is its fairness, its justice, its righteousness; the mere question of expediency and popularity does not enter. Only by the honest votes of good men can moral considerations obtain sway in political affairs. As a believer in God and in his kingdom the Christian citizen must endeavor to enact and execute laws which shall be the transcript of the writing on the adamant tables. A law that is simply the will of the majority speaks with no deep tone of authority and commands little reverence. But law becomes majestic, when it is regarded not as a mere conventional arrangement adopted by a majority vote, but as an expression of the will and righteousness of God.

The believer in God must do what lies in his power to secure the dominance of moral principles in civil affairs; he must seek to establish and maintain in human relations the justice of God; the life and law of that kingdom which is over all are to color all his thoughts, determine every duty, and be supreme in every part of life. We mean this: that social customs are to be inspired, legislative halls to be motived, national policies to be dictated, the nation's conscience to be enlightened by the great eternal principles of the kingdom of God—righteousness, and peace and gladness in the Holy Spirit.

Every man who sees a wrong and knows the right has a divine calling to follow the right and refuse the wrong. The world is full of men who lament the evils of politics, but will do nothing to improve things. The true citizen must do more than lament; he must go to work for the redemption of political life. The world is full of men, like Nicodemus, who are interested in everything that makes for salvation and for righteousness, but they do all their talking under cover of the night; they never raise their voices in brave protest and appeal. On the other hand, indiscriminate censure and scorn do little good. It is comparatively easy to

> " Say to the court, it glows
> And shines like rotten wood;
> Say to the church, it shows
> What's good, but does no good.

> If church and court reply,
>   Then give them both the lie."

Tennyson is right:

"It is better to fight for the good than to rail at the ill."

The man who believes in a better social order must show his faith by his works; he must be willing to endure some of the strain and pain and struggle of the kingdom. The man who believes in the good has a divine and urgent calling to strive for that good. The man who sees an evil without striving against it has denied the faith. A young man long ago went up to Jerusalem once upon a time to attend the Passover. He was an unknown peasant without following, without authority from any man, without any certificate of appointment from Cæsar or Sanhedrin. When he came to the temple set apart for the worship of Jehovah, he saw it profaned with all kinds of unlawful things. He saw men buying and selling right in the sacred precincts; he saw the court full of animals and crowded with tables of money changers. No doubt thousands of men before him had seen all this and had gone home lamenting it; they no doubt had declared that something ought to be done to remedy these great abuses. But it was none of their business, was it? See this one, however, gathering up the bits of rope lying around; see him knotting them into a whip; see his flashing eye and stern face as he advances on the crowd of temple desecrators; hear his ringing words: "Take these things hence." Jesus saw the wrong and he knew the right, and he felt the call of God within his soul to oppose the wrong and to uphold the right. Every citizen who sees a wrong has a divine call to rebuke and oppose it. Many excuse themselves on the ground that it is none of their business; they are not public officials; so they do nothing but criticise the public officials for failing in their duty. But it needs to be remembered that each citizen in a popular government is a public officer, and has official duties. The people are the kings, the authorities, the sovereigns.

I know very well what many men say to all this: They, the politicians and the groundlings, call it "Sunday School Politics." Perhaps it is, but it is none the worse for that. At any rate any other politics than this is an offense against the state, a sin against God, a treason to every high interest of humanity. The groundling politicians will object to all this; they will tell us that we are meddlers; they will have much to say about the dangers of religious interference in matters of state; they will tell us that we are getting out of our sphere. But the man who believes in God and has had a vision of the kingdom knows what is expected of him; he knows that he has a divine calling to go out into the world and seek in all ways to prepare for this kingdom. The man who believes in God can never get out of his sphere. The man who has a vision of the New City with its streets of gold, its water of life, its peace, its security, its righteousness, that city into which nothing enters that defiles, or works abomination, or makes a lie, sees that he is called to make these cities of earth more heavenly, more righteous, more peaceful and secure; he is summoned to cast out of these earthly cities everything that here defiles, or works abomination, or makes a lie. No man has any reason to suppose that he will ever be permitted to walk the streets of the New City till he has done something to make the streets and lanes of his native city purer and safer and more heavenly. Of course all this means effort and toil; it means that one will be misunderstood and abused; that one's peace will often be disturbed and one's soul will often be shaken. But, then, what is one here for? The New Citizen seeks a city, a city that has foundations, whose maker and builder is God. He seeks a city here below that shall be the copy and realization of the city above. He believes in a new earth in which dwelleth righteousness. And in all ways open to him as a man, as a citizen, he seeks to make the kingship of Jesus Christ real in human affairs. On the walls of the Signoria Palace in Florence is an inscription, placed there three hundred years ago by the Mayor, Niccolo Capprivi. It records how in the city council, and afterwards in the public assembly of the citizens, the people of Florence solemnly elected Jesus Christ king of the city and pledged themselves to be loyal to him.

Jesus
Christus Rex Gloriæ, venit in pace :
Christus vincit : Christus regnat :
Christus imperat :
Christus, ab omni malo nos defendat.*

That was a formal, external transaction and availed little. The mere insertion of the name of God in the Constitution, the mere acknowledgment of his authority over the state, avails little now. His is a reign of ideals and not of edicts ; his kingdom is not a matter of written constitutions, majority votes, and territorial boundaries ; it is a kingdom of righteousness, and peace, and gladness in the Holy Spirit. The kingdoms of this world become the kingdom of our God by the assimilation of their life into the life of the kingdom, and the transformation of their institutions into the ideals of the kingdom.

---

* Jesus
Christ, the King of Glory, comes in peace :
Christ conquers, Christ reigns :
Christ rules :
Christ from every evil defend us.

CHAPTER XI.

THE PALACE BEAUTIFUL.

But thou shalt call thy walls Salvation, and thy gates Praise.— THE PROPHET ISAIAH.

This is the perfect notion of a Christian church, that it should be a sovereign society, operating therefore with full power for raising its condition, first morally, and then physically ; operating through the fullest development of the varied faculties and qualities of its several members, and keeping up continually, as the bond of its union, the fellowship of all its people with one another through Christ, and their communion with him as their common head.— THOMAS ARNOLD.

The spiritual life, as the realization of the Christ-life, is not an inward regard, cherishing a private good, but an outward clasping, the showing of the mastery of the divine life in us by our ministration especially unto the least, the poorest, the most unlovely. If we have set out to find the palace of our King, resolving that we will enter it and live with him, even as the most abject of minions, we are not in the right way, and shall never see the palace nor find the King. He is serving our poor brothers in wretched hovels, numberless and near at hand, and if we will join him in this service, we shall find him there, and every hovel will seem unto us his palace.—*God in His World : An Interpretation.*

ON his way up the Hill Difficulty Bunyan's Pilgrim sees an arbor made by the Lord of the Hill for the refreshment of weary travelers. Here he turns in to rest, and here he loses his roll. After a time some one awakens him, saying : " Go to the ant, thou sluggard : consider her ways and

THE PALACE BEAUTIFUL. 261

be wise." In his confusion and haste Pilgrim forgets his roll, and goes on without it. Soon with many bitter regrets he retraces his way to the arbor seeking his precious roll. "But who can tell how joyful this man was when he had gotten his roll again ? For this roll was the assurance of his life, and acceptance at the desired haven." Thus he went on his way, till he beheld a very stately palace before him, of which the name was Beautiful; and it stood by the highway. This Palace Beautiful Pilgrim enters and is lovingly welcomed and kindly treated. Here he is greatly refreshed by a bountiful supper, and is greatly edified by the conversation of the guests. Two days he remains here, receiving much instruction concerning the Lord and the worthy doings of his servants of all ages. On the third day he is taken to the top of the Palace, where he is given a view of the Delectable Mountains in Immanuel's Land. Before starting out on his journey the residents of the Palace take him into the armory and equip him from head to foot with all the armor and all the weapons of a soldier. So refreshed, instructed and armed he proceeds on his way.

Of the three human institutions which are here by divine appointment, two are more or less involuntary; that is, membership in them is largely hereditary and compulsory. As we did not choose our family relations at birth, so very few voluntarily choose their civil relations. A man may pass from nation to nation, but he must go out of the world to get out of human society. The third institution, the church, is no less essential to man's largest and fullest life than the family and the state, but it is pre-eminently a voluntary society. What is the place which this institution fills in the development of life? And what is the claim which it makes upon men? These are real and practical questions, and a right answer to them may be helpful to the New Citizen.

I. THE CHURCH IS THE CONFESSION OF THE DIVINE LIFE IN MAN.

All of man's knowledge comes to fruitage in action. No man can know God, and Jesus Christ whom he has sent, without being greatly affected by that knowledge. For the Christian conception of God is that of an essentially moral being, and this means something to man. The man who sees that God is holy finds in that fact an urgent call: "Be ye also holy." The new spiritual life that one gains in Jesus Christ is not a possession which the individual can enjoy off in a corner by himself. To believe in Christ is to accept his life as the law of one's life, and to give up the will to his mastership. To heed his teachings, to follow him, is to enter into his conception of life, and act according to his will.

A man who has entered into this new life cannot be hid. The moment a candle is lighted it begins to radiate the light. It is the nature of light to shine, and the only way to dim the radiance is to quench the candle. Of the Lord Jesus we read: "He could not be hid." Nor can any man in whom he dwells. The first duty of every man who has this new life is to acknowledge and confess it. Jesus made much of this duty of confession: "Ye are the light of the world." "Let your light so shine before men that they may see your good works, and glorify your Father which is in heaven" (Matt. v. 14, 15). "If any man would come after me, let him deny himself, and take up his cross daily, and follow me" (Luke ix. 23). "Whosoever, therefore, shall confess me before men, him will I confess also before my Father which is in heaven. But whosoever shall deny me before men, him will I also deny before my Father which is in heaven" (Matt. x. 32, 33). The moment we stop to consider these words, that moment we see how reasonable and inevitable they are. The man who refuses to confess this new spiritual life thereby shows one of two things: Either he does not possess it; or he has it in an unworthy and perverted form. The man who is ashamed of Christ either does not know Christ, or he is unworthy of him. The man who really knows Christ can no more be ashamed of him, than the rose can be ashamed of the sunbeam which gives it color.

The nature of the spiritual life makes this confession of it necessary. The nature of the American spirit determines the form of the American citizenship. The man who has entered into the spirit of the American nationality is drawn to the American people ; he confesses his allegiance in his acts ; he accepts the claims and responsibility of his new position. The possession of the American spirit, by the very nature of the case, brings a man into relations with other persons who possess the same spirit. His citizenship is not something which he can hide in a napkin or under a bushel. That spirit, that citizenship, finds expression in a corporate body we call the American state. In the same way the man who possesses the spiritual life of Christ is, by the nature of the case, brought into certain relations with all other persons who have the same life.

A man's faith shows itself in his life. No man can believe in the sovereignty of Jesus Christ without seeking to put away all known sin. The spirit of Christ is the spirit of brotherhood, of loving fellowship, of kindly service, of social helpfulness. Horace Bushnell speaks of men who are fawning about the cross hoping to get some private token of grace, without suffering any experience, making any self-denial, or confessing any allegiance. Such men want to be saved by a fraud, by some secret experience which makes no open testimony and costs no sacrifice. Such men think only of themselves, and have no regard for the real spirit of the Christian life. The church stands before men as the organized and visible witness to Jesus Christ and his truth. It is a witness to the world of the divine Fatherhood and the human brotherhood.

The church is the realization of the brotherhood of man, and is the abiding witness to this truth in the face of all the rivalries and divisions of men. The man in whom the new life dwells, by a necessary attraction is drawn toward all other men who possess the same life. He acknowledges them as brothers in the new life; he identifies himself with them in their efforts and prayers; he says: Your honor shall be my concern; your cause shall be my cause; your Lord shall be my Lord. In this institution or society we call the church, we find the corporate and visible confession of this new life in man. "We cannot see the difference between right and wrong, between the purity, the kindness, and generosity, and love of Christ, and the uncleanness, and brutality, and cruelty, and hatefulness of sin, and remain utterly unmoved. We cannot stand in the midst of the mighty, world-historic conflict, where, on the one side, multitudes of men and women are being betrayed, and maltreated, and plundered by the sin of others; and, on the other side, thousands and tens of thousands of the best and noblest men and women the world has produced, are banded together in the name of Christ, in the endeavor, first, to banish sin from their own hearts and lives, and then to banish it from the hearts and lives of others, and so remove it from the world; we cannot stand emotionless between these contending hosts" (Hyde: Outlines of Social Theology, p. 118). The church, alas, we confess has not always been true to its calling;

there have been times when the churches hardly lisped the first syllable of the divine love and helpfulness ; there have been times when, as Professor Bruce says, men have been compelled to leave the church to remain Christians ; but in a large sense, the churches represent Jesus Christ, his truth, his cause, his brotherhood, his love, as no other institution or society. Perfect or imperfect as the churches may be, they are the organized confession of faith in Christ ; and confession of faith in Christ means also identification of one's self with the people of God. The man who thinks : " I am an American in spirit," but never identifies himself with the American people, never fulfills one act of American citizenship, never makes the problems and hopes of the American people his problems and hopes, who, in the hour of America's need and danger, stands aloof and raises no voice in her behalf and makes no sacrifice, is obviously unworthy of America, and must be put down as a man of alien spirit. As Horace Bushnell has shown : He that knows God will confess him. He says : " This matter of professing Christ appears to be regarded by many as a kind of optional duty. Just as optional as it is for light to shine, or goodness to be good, or joy to sing, or gratitude to give thanks, or love to labor and sacrifice for its ends. No ! my friends, there is no option here, save as all duties are optional and eternity hangs on the options we make." " We know," says the beloved disciple, " that we have passed from death unto life, because we love the brethren; he that loveth not his brother abideth in death."

II. THE CHURCH IS THE CO-OPERATION OF MEN IN BEHALF OF HOLINESS.

Man is by nature a social being. Sin is selfishness; it is the undue assertion of self. Conversion is the turning of the soul to God; the re-entrance of man into the true and divine life; it is the birth of the soul into the life of brotherhood. Now, for the first time, the man truly and rightly appreciates those ties which link him with his fellows. He learns how dependent he is upon his fellows, and how much they need his help. In the church he finds the organ of this common life, the medium of this mutual service.

Man is a being of relationships. He cannot come to perfection through isolation. The church is a body fitly framed together and compacted through every joint of the supply, according to the working in due measure of each single part, and effects the increase of the body unto the building up of itself in love (Eph. iv. 16). Through fellowship man enters into fullness of life. No man can gain the fullness of truth in isolation. The perfectly universal man has not yet been born. Men have different temperaments, and different aptitudes; they approach the truth through different avenues; the truth comes to them through different channels. Matthew and John walked and talked with the same Jesus; but each man saw that life at a different angle. Each man's picture of the Christ is true to reality, but their books represent different angles of observation. It has been pointed out that there were three schools of thought in the early church : the Johannean, the Pauline, the Petrine. All careful students of the Scriptures will admit that not one piece of writing can be spared from the New Testament. All these various writers, emphasizing various aspects of Christ's life and truth, are necessary to the full-rounded gospel of the Son of man. As the revelation has been given by divers portions and in divers manners, so it has become known in divers portions and through divers personalities. Scripture has a marvellous self-evidencing, self-interpreting power. But after all, the man who reads the Scriptures alone without help of any kind from other men must say as did the Ethiopian : "How can I understand these words unless some man guide me?" Through association men gain the full-rounded view of gospel truth. He is a foolish man who shapes his life by the opinions and views of other men. But he is no less vain and presumptuous who scorns and ignores the views and experiences of other disciples.

Again : through fellowship Christian worship is promoted and intensified. Public social worship is quite essential to the very existence of religious worship. Every religion the world has known has had its public gatherings for worship, sacrifice and prayer. It is possible for a man to live in isolation and preserve his faith in God. But the divine life, kept in isolation unsupported by sympathy, tends to languish and die. Suppose all the churches of a community were permanently closed ; suppose that each man resolved to withdraw into himself and to nourish his spiritual life in isolation. One does not need to be told what the result would be ; the almost total drying up of religion in that community, a waning consciousness of God and a loosening bond of brotherhood. As the reservoir that supplies the city with water becomes dry when all the supply springs are cut off ; so the spiritual life of the community languishes when the springs of fellowship are dried. All churches are no doubt very imperfect institutions, feebly, haltingly realizing the ideal of the Founder ; but imperfect as they are, they voice the universal longings of the human heart, they become a medium for the expression of religious worship, they nourish in the community the consciousness of God.

It is worthy of note that the promise of Christ's personal presence with his people finds its first fulfillment in the social gathering. Where two or three are gathered together in his name, there he promises to be present. It is worthy of note also that the Holy Spirit, God's best gift, comes in fullness and power upon the gathering of disciples. It was when they were all together, with one accord, in one place, that the Holy Spirit was poured out upon them. From the New Testament record one is warranted in saying that no man in isolation can receive the Holy Spirit in fullness. The Holy Spirit is a social spirit. He comes to men when heart is right with heart; he binds men together in loving fellowship; he moves men to serve one another in the spirit of Christ Jesus. The outpouring of the Spirit on Pentecost transformed that company of disciples into a Christian church, making them conscious now of their life in Christ and of their fellowship with one another. "In one Spirit were we all baptized into one body" (1 Cor. xii. 13). The baptism of water marks the formal introduction of the believer into the church; but this is the symbol, not the substance (Gordon: The Ministry of the Spirit, p. 55). The Holy Spirit is the realization of the life of God in the life of humanity. He comes to bind God and men together in a solidarity of life and fellowship. And what we call the church is this social realization of the life of God in the life of humanity.

This comparison of the church to a body is more than a happy comparison; it expresses a deep and vital fact. The member exists for the sake of the body, and he finds his fullest life through the body. We are but members, and shall never attain to the dignity of being a complete body in ourselves. We find our life as we lose our life in the life of the body. A man says: "I can read a better sermon at home than I can hear in the church; why then should I go to the church gathering?" His contention is just this far; he can read a better sermon than he can hear; but hearing good sermons is only a part of the church worship. The quickening of soul through fellowship; the answer of heart to heart in prayer, the uplift of soul through united song and praise, these are also necessary elements of the religious life. Another man says: "I can best commune with the eternal Spirit out in the fields or in the woods. I find more uplift of soul, more quickening of faith there than within the narrow walls of the meeting-house." Here and there may be a soul, half mystic, half philosopher, who realizes these words. But the average man or woman finds most uplift, most inspiration, most help in the social gathering of kindred souls. Those who forsake the assembling of themselves together will, as a rule, find great difficulty in maintaining their spiritual life. The testimony on this point is familiar to all. Men need the *feel* of belonging to a great body; Paul's spirit fainted within him as he waited at Athens alone.

And once more, the church is the medium of mutual service and sacrifice. The church is a fellowship in which the strong and the weak are brought together in brotherly relations. It is a confession of mutual dependencies and of mutual needs. The strong assume the obligation to help the weak and to bear their burdens. In every church are to be found disciples at all grades of attainment in the divine life. There are to be found in every church the strong and good, the pure, the godly, the unselfish, disciples of mature years and manly powers. And there are to be found also the weak, the laggards, the lapsed, the ignorant, the babes and nurslings of the family. By the nature of the fellowship the combined forces that make for good are at the disposal of the backward and the weak. The good and strong are to buttress and help the laggard and fallen. The whole helpfulness and philanthropy of Jesus Christ represented in that gathering are to be distributed over the whole company. And the resources of the saints are to be put to the widest use. Those who are strong and instructed must never say: We must part company with these laggards and weaklings; we will make a church for ourselves, and will allow them to exercise the same privilege in some other association. To do that is to deny utterly the Christ spirit, and is to make the church into a social club or a company of self-righteous Pharisees. "We then that are strong ought to bear the infirmities of the weak, and not to please ourselves." To bear one another's burdens is to fulfill the law of Christ. The fact is, however, there is no man who is wholly complete in himself. Each man needs to be buttressed at some point by his fellows; each man stands in need of some brother's grace and strength. The church is a household of faith, a family of children; but it is not a household of elder brothers to be feasted and robed and ringed; rather it is a household which imposes upon each member the task of welcoming home returning brothers with love and joy. In every church worthy of the name each member watches over his brother members, and is watched over by them in turn. Each man looks not alone on the things of self, but each man also on the things of others. Each man bears the burdens of others and so fulfills the law of Christ. The church is not a clique of the select, not a social club; but a home of loving ministry, of redemptive healings, of mutual service and sacrifice.

III. THE CHURCH IS THE ORGANIZED SERVICE OF THOSE WHO POSSESS THE SPIRITUAL LIFE IN CHRIST.

For the sake of the highest efficiency in service men need some such organization as the church. No man's life is so efficient as when it is joined to another life toward a common end. Did you ever go down into the cellar in the night to get some coal or to find an apple? You struck a match, but alas, after flickering a moment it went out. You did not throw away that most worthless thing, a burned match stick. No, you struck the other match and laid the burned stick alongside it, and thus had light for your purpose. In God's arithmetic twice one equals ten. One man in whom the Spirit dwells shall chase a thousand, and two shall put ten thousand to flight. Two men working together can accomplish far more than the same two men working separately. The difference in efficiency and power between a mob and an army is not in numbers nor in courage, but in organization. In war-times a man's heart may be full of patriotism, he may shoulder a musket and go forth against the enemy. But his patriotism and zeal avail little; he may harass the enemy but he wins no battles, and ends no war. One hundred regular soldiers will put to rout a thousand unorganized Indians, not because they are braver or better armed, but because they are organized.

The church is the body of Christ set here to serve and save the world. In the days of his flesh the Lord Jesus gave himself in all that he was and in all that he had for men. His feet took him on errands of mercy; his hands were employed in touching and healing the sick; his ears were open to the cries of need; his lips spoke words of cheer and hope; his eyes searched out the lost and his heart breathed out its prayer for men. Those who possess the life of Christ are members of his body to be used as his directing spirit appoints. Such persons are to be the eyes of Christ, his hands, his feet, his ears, his lips, his heart. The Christian church is Christ continued, Christ carried along, and made permanent and visible and active among men. The church is Christian no farther than it is the organized and continuous sacrifice and passion of Christ. Each man has his own peculiar talent; the work for one man may not be the work for another. " God hath set some in the church, first apostles, secondly prophets, thirdly teachers, then miracles, then gifts of healings, helps, governments, divers kinds of tongues" (1 Cor. xii. 28, R. V.). There is work in the kingdom of God of all kinds, at all levels, for all sorts of talent. In the economy of the kingdom the work of the hand may be quite as necessary as that of the eye or tongue. The physician who applies nature's remedies and heals the sick is doing the work of the kingdom quite as truly as the evangelist or the prophet. The legislator who is working for better laws may be as truly a worker in the kingdom as the temperance advocate who seeks to save the drunkard. It is a Christly thing to minister to the half-dead traveler on the Jericho road, but it is quite as necessary that one seeks to break up that nest of robbers infesting that road. To nurse the fever-stricken man is a divine service; but is it any less divine to drain the quagmire in which the fever is bred? Is it not as Christly a thing to remove causes as to cure results? The church, the body of Christ, stands before the world as the living embodiment of his whole philanthropy and helpfulness. In the accomplishment of its work there is use for all sorts of talent and powers. There is no useless member in the body of Christ.

The church is not an end in itself; it has just one thing to do in this world; to be the continued incarnation of the Christ life; to glorify God and to seek his kingdom. The church is here to be the organ of the everlasting love of Christ for men, the agency for the promotion of his kingdom among men. We know how overwhelming is the power of the things that are outward and visible; how we become engrossed with material things; how the cares of this world and the deceitfulness of riches tend to enter in and choke the word. The church is a perpetual witness to the unseen and the eternal, and keeps alive in men the consciousness that they belong to another order. By the solemn assemblies for praise and prayer men are reminded of their dependence one upon another; and by their brotherly fellowship the world is given a lesson in the meaning of brotherly love. By the instruction imparted from the pulpit, in the Sunday-school, and in other ways, the righteous will of God is brought home to men's consciences and hearts. There is set up before the world another standard than the conventional and popular one; there is held up the standard of eternity, and men are summoned to test their lives by the requirements of the great white throne. By the ordinances of the church the world is given a visible illustration of the great realities of the Christian gospel. Whatever view may be held regarding baptism, one meaning cannot be overlooked. It is a pledge to the world that the person has entered into the life of Christ, and belongs to God. The apostle connects this splendid truth with baptism: " For as many of you as have been baptized into Christ, have put on Christ. There is neither Jew nor Greek, there is neither bond nor free, there is neither male nor female;

for ye are all one in Christ Jesus" (Gal. iii. 28). The other ordinance, the Lord's Supper, bears witness to a truth no less splendid and significant. And this truth is well expressed in the quaint words of Archbishop Cranmer : "For like as bread is made of a great number of grains of corn, ground, broken, and so joined together, that thereof is made one loaf ; and an infinite number of grapes be pressed together in one vessel, and thereof is made wine ; likewise is the whole multitude of true Christian people spiritually joined, first to Christ, and then among themselves, together, in one faith, one baptism, one Holy Spirit, one knot and bond." On its manward side this ordinance witnesses forever to the reality of the bond of brotherhood and love as the bond of the new society. It also erects a standard for the daily life and the common task, reminding us that life belongs to God and that we are to do all our eating and drinking in remembrance of Christ. No one can measure the power and influence of the church in the world. Says a strong writer : " Important as the Sabbath is as a means of rest and grace, a chief element of that importance is that it periodically invites the soul to vacate the sphere of worldly concerns and distractions, and washing from herself the accumulated grime of the week, enter the calm, pure, bracing air of the sanctuary, where she shall hear no sounds save such as echo the angelic. The chaste and consecrated temple, the gathered multitude, the devout posture, the humble invocation, the solemn Scriptural reading, the reverent adoration, the hearty thanksgiving, the lowly confession, the tender penitence, the fervent supplication, the glowing consecration, the large-hearted intercession, the ardent panting after God, the peaceful communion with him, the uplifting sermon, the melody of hymn and chant, of voice and organ, the solemn baptismal vow, the blissful banquet of the Holy Communion—these are the stately buttresses and graceful shafts on which Christ rests the temple of his truth and grace, and from which his righteousness goeth forth as brightness, and his salvation as a lamp that burneth" (George Dana Boardman : Studies in the Mountain Instruction, p. 71).

Under the terms of three striking figures the Master has set forth the mission of his church in the world. The disciples are as light in the world, bearing witness for the truth, enlightening the conscience of men, making men know what is that good and acceptable and perfect will of God. They are the salt of the earth, purifying, sweetening, preserving the life of mankind from decay and death, and making it meet for the Master's use. They are like the leaven hidden in the meal, to transform and change it, and make it fit for the Master's table. The church is not a mutual benefit society, though it benefits in incalculable ways its members. It is not a social club, though its social life is most marked. Over and above all this, it is a society intent on the one object of purifying, sweetening, transforming, saving, the entire life of the world. "The true and grand idea of a church," said Thomas Arnold, "is a society for making men like Christ, earth like heaven, and the kingdoms of this world the kingdom of our God."

The light is to illuminate and reveal; the salt is to preserve and sweeten something; the leaven is to leaven and change and transform the mass of meal. The meeting-house of the church is the class-room of the King's children, the place where they are instructed in the will and way of God. That meeting-house is the mountain-top where visions of life are shown the builders of God's tabernacle among men. It is the drill-room of the King's soldiers, where they meet and plan campaigns. It is the upper room where the risen Christ comes to breathe upon his disciples and to commission them for their work. It is the family room where the Father's children meet to talk over their common hopes, and to pray and plan how to help and save their wayward brothers. In a word, these instructed, inspired, trained, commissioned disciples, when the service in the meeting-house is over, arise and go out to serve their fellows in every way possible, and to seek the kingdom in every way open. Jesus Christ came not to be ministered unto but to minister, and to give his life a ransom for many. The church is true to its Lord in so far as it fulfills this same loving ministry. Its one only business in the world is to bring the world to Jesus Christ. Spurgeon has said: "A church is a soul-saving community, or it is nothing." The church that ceases to be missionary has ceased to be Christian. This word "missionary" is as wide as the human race and as deep as human need. In the program of the kingdom there are no home missions, no foreign missions. The disciples are sent into the world to minister to every creature who needs their help and whom they can reach. Neighborhood is not a matter of distance but of need and ability. The church is Christ's representative in the world, the pillar and ground of the truth, the channel and medium of his saving grace to a lost world. Some one has put this truth in the following form. Jesus Christ, at his ascension after his passion and resurrection, is greeted at the gate of heaven as a glorious victor. Cherubim cry: "Lift up your heads, O ye gates; even lift them up, ye everlasting doors, and the King of glory shall come in." And seraphim chant in antiphone: "Who is this King of glory?" And all heaven joins in the hallelujah chorus: "The Lord who all his foes o'ercame." Finally, Gabriel inquires of the Lord of glory in whose care he has left his work on earth. And the King replies: "With Peter and the other disciples." "But suppose these men should fail to do this work?" And the King replied: "I have made no other arrangements."

CHAPTER XII.

GAINING THE CROWN.

He that is faithful in a very little is faithful also in much : and he that is unrighteous in a very little is unrighteous also in much.—JESUS CHRIST.

The earth is no sojourn of expiation. It is the home wherein we are to strive towards the realization of that ideal of the true and just, of which each man has in his own soul the germ. It is the ladder towards that condition of perfection which we can only reach by glorifying God in humanity, through our own works, and by consecrating ourselves to realize in action all that we may be of his design.—JOSEPH MAZZINI.

The whole substance of religion was faith, hope and love ; by the practice of which we become united to the will of God : that all beside is indifferent, and to be used as a means that we may arrive at our end, and be swallowed up therein, by faith and love.
That all things are possible to him who believes—that they are less difficult to him who hopes— that they are more easy to him who loves, and still more easy to him who perseveres in the practice of these three.—BROTHER LAWRENCE.

> When wealth is lost, nothing is lost ;
> When health is lost, something is lost ;
> When character is lost, all is lost.
> —*Motto on the Wall of a German School.*

ONE day at sea a man in a little open boat was overtaken by a storm, and his vessel was wrecked ; hungry, cold, and naked he was cast upon an island. Soon he saw a crowd of natives coming up in high glee. "I have escaped the sea," thought the man, "only to die a miserable death on land." But no, the natives picked him up kindly, carried him to their city, clothed him, placed a crown on his head, and seated him on a throne. Then they stood around in respectful silence awaiting his orders. "This," thought the man, "is but the insane ceremony that precedes my destruction." But no harm befell him, and he found that these men were ready to serve his every wish. Finally, he inquired of an old man the meaning of all this. The old man gave this explanation: "You are our king, and we are here to fulfill your orders to the last letter." And so it proved: the natives were ready to carry out his commands and to do his orders. Several months went by; one day the king chanced to meet the old man once more, and now he asked a full explanation of this strange condition. "There is nothing strange about it; you are our king; each year a man is thrown upon our coast and we pick him up and do with him as we have done with you." "But," inquired the man, "what has become of your late king?" The old man went on: "As we find him naked, so at the end of the year we strip him of his royal apparel, put him in a boat and send him away to an island beyond the horizon, where we suppose he perishes." "And will you do so with me?" asked the king. "Yes."

When the king heard this he at first determined to spend the remainder of his time eating and drinking. But soon wiser and better thoughts came. Once more he sought out the old man. "Am I king now?" "Yes," answered the old man. "And can I do as I will?" "Absolutely," replied the old teacher. "Then," said the king, "I will spend the remainder of my time in fitting up that desolate island beyond the horizon." So he began transporting to it buildings, food, clothing, everything that he would need. The year ran out; the king was dethroned, stripped of his royal trappings, placed in a boat, and sent away to that island beyond. But there he found a welcome and a home, the welcome and a home which he himself had provided.

This parable, whose authorship is unknown, best lets us into the heart of this concluding chapter of our study. We are here as kings, crowned and placed over the things of God's hand. Soon we shall be stripped of these royal trappings and shall go hence. Here arises the problem of man's life: to see the high possibilities of present opportunities; to convert material resources into spiritual potencies; and to take with him into the unseen the full results and equivalents of his life on earth.

I. THE MAKING OF CHARACTER IS THE MEANING OF LIFE.

James Martineau has said that there are three kinds of human distinction: some men are eminent for what they *possess;* some for what they *achieve;* others for what they *are.* "Having, Doing, and Being, constitute the three great distinctions of mankind, and the three functions of their life." This most luminous writer then goes on to analyze somewhat more in detail these three kinds of distinction. In every community there are many people who derive their chief distinction from what they have; they are always spoken of in terms of revenue. In themselves, detached from their possessions, they would be neither eminent nor winning. When these men die, the mammon image cannot be removed, and it is the fate of the money and not of the man of which men are most apt to think. Without in any way ignoring or belittling the proper acquisition of wealth, it must be evident to all that having is not the great distinction in life. Of the men who have lived to accumulate and to enjoy, history is for the most part silent. History, on the other hand, is the record rather of what man has attempted and achieved, and the record is a long and glorious one, of ease surrendered for conflict, of labor for the welfare of others, of wealth sacrificed for liberty. There on history's pages shine the names of the men who have broken the tents of ease and have advanced to the dangers of lonely enterprise and to conflict with entrenched wrong; men who have thrown reputation and fortune and life into the issue, and have toiled and spent themselves in the campaign for justice and truth and liberty. We may know regret over the grave of the Epicurean, but we weep over the grave of the hero.

"But there is a life higher than either of these. The saintly is beyond the heroic. To get good is animal: to do good is human: to be good is divine" ("Endeavors after the Christian Life"). That is to say, character is finer, higher, worthier than wealth or honor. Character is as much finer than either possessions or achievements as the man is higher than anything he possesses or does. The man is the chief thing.

> "The rank is but the guinea-stamp,
> The man's the gowd for a' that."

And character is something which exists entirely independent of the accessories and accidents of life. A man may wear a crown of gold and be called King Agrippa, and possess no character worthy of any honor. A man may be a pale and wasted prisoner, with manacled hands, and faded cloak, and may be known as Paul the prisoner; but he may have a character that shines resplendent as the stars. Here comes out that well-known distinction between reputation and character. Reputation is an accessory of life; it is what men think us to be. Character is an elemental fact of life, and is what God knows us to be. This is the real measure of the man. A man may be poorly dressed as Socrates; he may live in a wilderness, as John the Baptist; he may be a peasant's son, as Martin Luther; he may be a poor cobbler, as William Carey; and the world will acknowledge his kingship, and will be moved by the force of his character. "Character teaches over our heads," says Emerson. Again he says that those who listened to Lord Chatham felt that there was something finer in the man than anything he said. "You could not stand with Burke under an archway while a shower of rain was passing," said Samuel Johnson, "without discovering that he was an extraordinary man." "This," says Emerson, "is what we call character, a reserved force which acts directly by presence and without means." "Oh, Iole, how did you know that Hercules was a God?" "Because I was content," answered Iole, "the moment my eyes fell on him. When I beheld Theseus I desired that I might see him offer battle, or at least guide his horses in the chariot race; but Hercules did not wait for a contest; he conquered whether he stood, or walked or sat, or whatever he did" (Emerson: Essays, Character). Call it what we will, character, personality, holiness, there is something in right being which attracts, moves, wins, compels men. "In him was life, and the life was the light of men." No preacher's sermon is one half as powerful as himself; it is the man that gives the sermon weight and authority.

The making of character, we say, is the meaning of life. Character is a creation of one's own efforts. We begin life innocent; we become either sinful or holy. We begin life weak and ignorant, a bare possibility: we make either good character or bad. That is to say, character is an achievement. We are given a name at birth : men determine more or less our reputation ; but we make the worth of our name ; we ourselves make or mar our characters. There is no power outside the man himself that can mar his character, as there is no power that can alone make his character. Character is the result of our choices, the weight of our personality, the thing that we have made ourselves. The highest good that can ever come to a man in this world or in any world is a good that can be read in terms of character. The grace of God that bringeth salvation has appeared that we might become gracious. Jesus Christ is blessing and saving a man just so far as the man is being conformed to the character and image of Christ. Men see Christ's face when they have his character. Men are all too apt to look abroad for good, and to expect blessedness in a change of condition. But the only true good is within, and the only blessedness which Christ has pronounced is the blessedness of character. The crown which the disciple gains is a crown of *life*. Right life is itself the crown of glory. There is no crown for those who have not won the crown of right character. "His servants shall do him service ; and they shall see his face ; and his name—that is his character, shall be on their foreheads."

II. THE WORLD IS DESIGNED FOR THE MAKING OF CHARACTER.

We come into the world weak, limited, ignorant.

All that we ever know we must learn for ourselves. There is no such thing as inherited wisdom, experience, or character. We sometimes ask in perplexity: Why did not God make us creatures of a longer sight, a wider knowledge, a larger being? Earth might have been without any darkness, life might have had no mysteries, the way of duty might have been perfectly plain. Why has God placed us in this world of sorrow, of danger, of trial, of struggle? Because he values character, and character can only be made and tested in trial and struggle and danger. Men ask: Is this the best possible world? Without hesitation we answer: Yes, for the purpose that God has in view. Things are so arranged in this world that character must be made and tested. God wants man to grow, to become strong, to achieve a victory, to win a character. So all around are difficulties to rouse him to effort; there are mysteries to provoke him to study; there are two ways open to awaken moral consciousness. Before him various roads are open, and he is in danger of turning into the wrong path. Thus there must be a forecasting of results, a choice of roads, a moral discrimination. The very difficulty and hardness of man's lot call out all his hidden capabilities; the very struggle puts fire into his eye and iron into his blood; it creates and develops moral character.

This life from beginning to end is man's schoolhouse. No one ever gets beyond his school days. He may pass from room to room, but he never

GAINING THE CROWN. 289

passes out of the school of life. The child begins life ignorant of the properties of things around it; so each soul must begin with the alphabet of experience. When the child is grown he must live among hard, material things; so early he must learn the properties of matter. By falls he learns that the floor is hard, and will not yield. He discovers that his head and the door cannot occupy the same space at the same time. The knife cuts, the fire burns, gravitation must not be left out of account. The pupil going to school finds his lessons hard, and the lesson advances with the advance of the pupil. When these problems in arithmetic are worked out, what is the answer worth? But the discipline has done the boy untold good. Some time grammar-school days will be over, the boy will become a man, and will have a man's problems to solve. At every step he is confronted with problems which are not down in the books. According to the use he has made of his earlier years is he now able to meet and solve these problems. Every end is also a beginning. The experience of one stage prepares the soul for new problems, and the new problems make new experiences.

As it was better, youth
Should strive, through acts uncouth,
Toward making, than repose on ought found made:
So, better, age, exempt
From strife, should know, than tempt
Further. Thou waitedst age; wait death nor be afraid.
. . . .

He fixed thee mid this dance
Of plastic circumstance,
This present, thou, forsooth, wouldst fain arrest:
Machinery just meant
To give thy soul its bent,
Try thee and turn thee forth, sufficiently impressed.
(BROWNING: *Rabbi Ben Ezra*.)

Well might he say elsewhere:

Was the trial sore?
Temptation sharp? Thank God a second time!
Why comes temptation but for man to meet
And master and make crouch beneath his foot,
And so be pedestaled in triumph? Pray,
"Lead us into no such temptation, Lord!"
Yea, but O thou whose servants are the bold,
Lead such temptations by the head and hair,
Reluctant dragons, up to who dares fight,
That so he may do battle and have praise.
(*Ring and the Book: The Pope*.)

Life we say means character. This life may be a school, but it is a school in which an immortal soul is shaping an immortal character, and so an immortal destiny.

" Here sits he shaping wings to fly,
His heart forebodes a mystery,
He names the name, Eternity."

The lessons man learns in this school of life go into the molding and shaping of character. Changing the figure a little, we may say that life is a great mill and man is at the loom. At that loom he is weaving the fabric of character, a fabric that shall outlast the stars. The warp is laid of the many threads of circumstance, and condition, and providence; the woof is made of our choices and words and deeds. Back and forth flies the shuttle carrying the threads of our choices; the loom weaves on, the fabric grows, and lo, there is our life's pattern for the eye of the Master. Or, changing the figure once more, we may say that life is a workshop, in which man is framing the structure of noble character. The product of his planning and toil stands visible, by and by, in the majestic building fitly framed and compacted together by the harmonious combination of materials. But all the time he has been erecting another building that stands visible only to the eye that sees in secret. This invisible building is the counterpart of the visible building. Has the man put his best effort into this work; has he properly fitted every joint, has he scamped no hidden spot, has he done honest, faithful, conscientious work? If so, there are no ugly seams in his own character; his inner life is compact, honest, faithful, ready to meet the scrutiny of the Master Builder.

In Western New York, near the home of a gentleman of means, lived a poor family; the wife was industrious and deserving, but the husband was a shiftless carpenter. The gentleman one day determined to do something for this family; so, before going away for some months, he commissioned this do-little man to build a house on an indicated piece of ground. The gentleman's charge was:

"Build it well; do it as you would do if it were your own house." The man accepted the commission, but responsibility did nothing for him. He put poor material into the structure and charged for good; he scamped the joints, he took no pains to make the roof waterproof. But when finished it presented a good appearance with its puttied cracks and fresh paint. When the gentleman came home he inspected the work; without comment on the workmanship he said to the man: "This is your house; you have built it for yourself." In six months' time the man's unfaithfulness was all revealed to himself and to the world. The man's constant comment was this: "What a fool I was; if I had known this was to be my house, how differently I would have built it." The man who thinks he is cheating another is cheating himself. The mechanic who scamps his employer's house is more sadly scamping his own character. Fidelity is shown in little things, driving nails, weighing sugar, sweeping rooms, plowing fields, shifting railroad switches, writing books, preaching sermons. "He that is faithful in that which is least is faithful also in much; and he that is unjust in the least is unjust also in much."

Modern scientific thought has formulated what is called the law of the conservation and transformation of energy. Thus it is possible to transform friction into heat, and motion into light. But this law has innumerable applications. Coal, water, and iron are among the most inert and lifeless things in the world. Yet they may be so combined and transformed as to create energies and results higher than themselves. At one end of the process we have the coal and the water; at the other we have the electric current and the flashing light. The strength of the wheatfield appears in the vigorous right arm. In the last analysis it will appear that material things have value to man just so far as they can be transformed into mental and spiritual energies. Even economics go out into theology. In themselves oil and wheat have no value, but from what they will accomplish they acquire an infinite value. And there are in these things higher possibilities than most men suppose. The Master has given a most striking parable of the shrewd but unjust steward who is about to be turned out of office. For a life of toil he declares he is unfitted, to beg he is ashamed. In his extremity a bright idea suggests itself: He will so manipulate the oil and wheat at his command as to make sure of future entertainment till he can adjust himself to the new conditions. Oil and wheat he converts into affection and gratitude. Between oil and affection there is no common standard of measurement, but this man changes one into the other. The end rolls round and the man goes out of office, to find that the resources which once he had managed continue to bless and serve him. And unjust as the transaction may have been in itself, his lord cannot but commend his shrewdness and insight.

He sees that present, material, temporal things have a future, spiritual, convertible value. The time is coming in every man's life when material things will no longer signify or serve. Happy is that man who has recognized the convertible and spiritual possibilities of material things, and has transformed them into higher and eternal terms. The accessories and accidents of life must all be left on this side of the grave; everything personal and essential, everything that has a real value goes with us. We come into the world a bare possibility; material resources come into our hands: we go hence soon and leave all these perishable and temporal things. Here is the problem of every man's life: to invest himself in priceless values, to convert material resources into spiritual potencies, to carry into eternity the full results and equivalents of the life on earth; in a word, to transform work into character, and material possibilities into spiritual characteristics. Man's work in the world consists in the spiritualizing, the eternizing of present resources and opportunities. The whole work of life consists in this "subliming of energy." "We brought nothing into this world," says the apostle, "and it is certain we can carry nothing out." In the sense in which the apostle used the words they are absolutely true. But there is a sense in which they are not true. Material resources we brought not with us, and we take not with us. But everything that is personal and essential to ourselves we take with us. We came into the world innocent and characterless; we go hence taking the character which we have won. And in that character it is possible for a man to take the conserved and transformed equivalent of all the material resources which have come into his hands. The maker of character must learn that this law of the conservation and transformation of energy reaches on and up into the realm of soul, and that there is such a thing as the transformation of daily work into eternal character. The Sandwich Islander believes that the strength of a conquered foe passes into the body of the conqueror. In moral and spiritual matters it is precisely so.

Character is an achievement. The man who meets and overcomes obstacles is a better man than the one who has never known difficulty. Strong character, worthy character, can be made and tested only in the face of strong obstacles. In the South Seas the conditions of life are most easy and hospitable, and man has nothing to do but reach out his hand and pluck the breadfruit from a tree; yet manhood is at a low plane, so low that human beings live but little above the level of the brutes. Scotland has neither a hospitable soil nor a hospitable climate, but it has something better : it has strong vigorous manhood. The struggle of life has developed man, and has produced a hardy and energetic race. Say what men will about the hardness of the law of the struggle for existence, where the struggle is keenest man is strongest. Only by hard labor can the majority of men win their support out of an unwilling earth. In close factories, over scorching furnaces, with tired body, heavy heart, and whirling brain, man must earn his living. Sometimes we are inclined to complain of all this and to chafe at our human lot. But the very hardness of man's lot develops energy of character, it calls out his hidden capabilities ; patience, perseverance, fidelity, become the crowning virtues of man.

> Life is not as idle ore,
> But iron dug from central gloom,
> And heated hot with burning fears,
> And dipped in baths of hissing tears,
> And battered with the shocks of doom
> To shape and use.
>
> TENNYSON : *In Memoriam*, cxvii.

There is no mistake about our human lot if we only look deep enough. The presence of sin in God's universe is a stupendous problem. God does not want it here, else he had not given his Son to put it away by the sacrifice of himself. Man does not want it. And sin is not desirable for its own sake. Yet it is here, a hard, stubborn, awful, fact, darkening man's life, and threatening his eternity. The origin and cause of sin we are not able to understand, and we must leave the problem for the present life. But now that sin is here, we can easily see that it may be a part of the education toward a worthier blessedness. The presence of sin exposes man to fearful risks, but were there no sin to be overcome there could be for man no right character achieved, no holy conscience won. Holiness can only be known as holiness in the face of things that offend and thwart it. Character can only be achieved in the presence of trial and toil. Does any one complain because God made him a man and will hold him responsible for his life? Who had rather be an innocent sheep, incapable of sin, and so incapable of holiness, than to be a man exposed to temptation, taking blows, enduring hardness, but capable of overcoming and gaining the crown of unfading glory? This we know: a man saved from sin is a grander, worthier man, than one who never was in danger. It is better to be a man and know the risk of failure and the privilege of character, than to be a sheep, and never know this risk and privilege. Some may fail; they may refuse the fight and shirk the toil and lose the crown. Were character to be gained by wishing, it would have no value. Only to the conquerors go the crowns. There is one song which even the angels cannot sing: it is the song of redeeming love. And grander, sweeter, worthier than the song of unfallen angels is the song of those who have come up through tribulation, and have washed their robes, and made them white in the blood of the Lamb.

> This world's no blot for us
> Nor blank; it means intensely, and means good.

What makes the hero? Calmness in the face of

danger. What makes the saint? Overcoming the world and one's own heart. What makes character such a priceless thing? The cost at which it must be won.

III. THE WELL-MADE CHARACTER IS FITTED FOR HIGH RESPONSIBILITIES.

Character is power for this world and for every world. Character is a timeless thing. It is the one thing that God values, the one thing that has meaning in the place of trade, in the pulpit, in the home, in the state, before the great white throne in the courts of heaven. The world is always looking for men of character, men whose opinions are not for sale; men who are sound from centre to circumference; men whose conscience is as steady as the needle to the pole; men who can suffer but cannot tell a lie; men who can look the devil in the face and tell him he is a devil; men who can stand for the right though the heavens fall; men who can die for the truth but cannot run from the wrong: men whose moral latitude and longitude can be forecast at any hour of the day or night; men who can be trusted without bond and can be faithful when no one sees. Character for this life is an end in itself; to be is its own reward. But character like godliness is profitable for the life that now is, and it contains a promise for the life that is to come.

The life of man was made for two worlds. The life here and the life there make up the sum of human existence. The sky of the most meagre human life overarches both time and eternity. We take ourselves with us wherever we go in time or in eternity; and character makes heaven, and the want of it hell. To make good character is why we are here. If we have failed in this we have failed all along the line; hopelessly, irreparably we have failed. In these few years of life men are determining their fitness or unfitness to be placed over larger responsibilities in the larger kingdom of heaven. Here we are as stewards handling the resources of another; but by the use of these temporal things we gain something for ourselves. Very significant is this word of the Lord Jesus as he sums up that parable of the shrewd steward: "If therefore ye have not been faithful in the unrighteous mammon, who will commit to your trust the true riches?" "And if ye have not been faithful in that which is another man's, who shall give you that which is your own?" The lesson is clear; as we use our present resources do we determine what shall be our future status and our future worth. According to the degree of fidelity shown here in the use of material things,—the unrighteous mammon,—do we determine our fitness for larger trusts in the future. In the Master's parable of the pounds we have the same truth from a different point of view. The man who has gained ten pounds is placed over ten cities. Man is a trader now, but he is to be a ruler by and by. The end that the noble lord has in view for these servants is not money-making but character-making. He wants to create in them a hardihood of temper, a firmness of will, an energy of thought, which can be turned to good account, when these traders have become rulers.

This universe is far greater than any of us suppose. What work there may be in store for the fitted men who can tell? What trusts are waiting high character we cannot imagine. But there is reason to believe, from the analogy of spirit, that what we call heaven is a realm of the most unceasing activity. Once men thought of the universe as finished; now through geology and astronomy we know that it is in process of making. What part the man of high character may be called to play in this great process, no one can say; but these considerations open before us a wide field for thought. Whatever may be the trust committed to the man of holy character, one thing is clear: the trust will be adjusted to the capacity and fidelity of the soul. Here men estimate the work and worth of man by artificial and arbitrary standards. Men divide work into high or low, more respectable or less respectable, noble or base. But in heaven's estimate such considerations do not obtain. Heaven's estimate takes note only of the fidelity shown, the patience, the love, diligence. "Life," said James Russell Lowell, "is constantly weighing us in very sensitive scales, and telling every one of us precisely what his real weight is to the last grain of dust." He who builds a structure to outlast the stars cannot too carefully scrutinize the materials used, nor can he too faithfully follow the pattern shown in the mount, nor too prayerfully keep his hand true to the highest fidelity.

> Build it well, whate'er you do;
> Build it straight, and strong, and true;
> Build it clean, and high, and broad.
> Build it for the eye of God.

INDEX.

	PAGE
Agassiz	133
Advantage, unfair	229
A Kempis	73
Alway, George	59
Ambition	160
Amiel	122, 164
Amusements	196
—— Questionable	196
—— Proper	198
Andrews, E. Benj.	226
Aristotle	191, 212, 232, 237, 245
Arnold, Thomas	22, 279
Art	30
Ascetic ideal	11
Asceticism	191
Augustine	59
Bascom, John	152, 154, 166
Beatific Vision	11
Bible, books of	63
—— Study of	137
Biography	69
Boardman, Geo. Dana	122, 278
Body of humanity	16
Books	141
Brainerd, David	101
Brooks, Phillips	232
Browning, Mrs	139
Browning, Robert	29, 38, 78, 134, 203, 290, 297
Bryce, James	12
Byron, Lord	37
Buddhist precept	29
—— Saint	26
Buffon	132
Bunyan, John	73, 188, 260
Burke, Edmund	46, 241, 242, 286
Burritt, Elihu	142
Bushnell, Horace	156, 264, 266
Cain	91
Caliph Ali	161
Calvin, John	13, 164
Carlo Borromeo	200
Carlyle, Thos.	69, 96, 194, 216, 221
Carpenter, W. B	129
Character	26, 286, 295
—— Balance in	145
—— Ideals of	7, 283
—— Natural	28
—— Progress of	19, 27
—— Supreme thing	285
Channing, W. E	160
China, Emperor of	227
Christ	5, 170
Christian	89
Christianity, a feast	192
—— Timeliness of	7
—— Reality of	23, 181
Church	262
—— A body	270
—— Business of	170
—— Christ continued	274
—— Household of faith	272
—— Importance of	269
—— Ordinances of	276, 279
—— Organized service	273
Cicero	229
Circe	198
City, seeking a	258
Citizenship	245
Clark, Prof. J. B	223, 228, 231
Clergy	12
Communion in prayer	108, 110
Coleridge, S. T	67, 119
Confession in prayer	107
Confessing Christ	263
Contentment	159
Creation, Christ in	76
Cross	74
—— Joy in	91, 93
—— Law of life	85, 93
—— Disciple's	86
—— Power of	92
Dale, R. W	22, 37, 194, 226

INDEX

	PAGE
Daniel	137
Dante	11
Democracy, drift toward	248
Destruction, city of	25
Dewey, Orville	217
Discipleship	87
Distinction, three kinds of	284
Dives	56
Doctrines	70
Drummond, Prof. Henry	5, 18, 47, 163, 182, 231
Earnings	224
Ecclesiastes	37
Economics	221
Egypt	49
Elisha	57
Eliot, George	131
Emerson, R. W.	286
Employer and employé	227
Energy, conservation of	292
Evil	151
Evils, list of	21
Excuses, common	205
Fable of the wind and sun	153
Fairbairn, Prin. A. M	167
Family	235
Farmer	183
Fénelon	141, 198
Fidelity shown	292
Findlay, G. G	172
Florence, Christ king of	258
Fremantle, Canon, W. H.	12, 13, 232, 233
Future world and work	300
Galatians, Epistle to	171
Gambling	226
Gentile prayer	116
Gilman, N. P.	222
God, ever present	53, 61, 62
— Sovereignty of	101
— Universal will	251
Good Samaritan	27
Gordon, A. J	270
Gordon, G. A	165
Gospels, four	66
Grace, growth in	19
Gregory the Great	28
Guizot	13
Habits	123
— And character	129
— Good	127
— Law of	124
— Mental	131
— Moral	133
— Permanence of	125
— Of prayer	136

	PAGE
Habits Of Bible study	137
— Of reading	140
— Of Christian service	139
Hamilton, Sir Wm	132
Hart, Prof. J. S	34
Hatch, Edwin	9, 10
Help, man needs	98
Hebrews, Epistle to	7, 71
Herbert, George	187
Hercules	286
Herron, George D	235
Herodotus	131
Hitchcock, R. D	84
Holiness	267
— to the Lord	269
Hodges, Dean George	5
Honors	58
Hosea	64
Hubmaier, B	13
Hudson River	94
Hugo, Victor	130
Humility	150, 157
Hyde, Pres. DeWitt	19, 105, 265
Ideals, varying	14
Idealist	36
Ignis Fatuus	40
Impatience	164
Indifference impossible	265
Industry, Captains of	233
Inertia	122
Inspiration	67
Institutions, three Divine	235, 261
Integrity	201
Jacob	68
James	114
Jehovah	52
Jesus among men	22
— Cleansing temple	256
Joan of Arc	44
Job	107
Joel, prophet	35
John, Apostle	87, 193
John, Baptist	55, 157
Johnson, Samuel	286
Jones, Mayor S. M	225
Joseph	200
Judaism	168
Keble	182
King and peasant	214
Kingdom of God	223
— Ideals of	247
Koran	214
Law in nature	54, 99, 103
Lawyer	184

INDEX.

	PAGE
Legislation	253
Leighton, Archbishop	80, 192
Lieber, Francis	253
Life a school	288
—— No mistake	296
—— Springs of	28
Longfellow	35
Love	77, 79
Lowell	17, 34, 45, 300
Luke's Gospel	65
Luther, Martin	13
Lubbock, Sir John	142
Macaulay, T. B.	191
Man discontented	59
—— For two worlds	293
Marshall, Alfred	221
Martineau, James	283
Martyn, Henry	145
Matheson, George	32, 111, 115, 167, 208
McClure, J. G. K.	44, 202
Mechanic	183
Merchant, calling	183
—— Saint	25
Mill, John S.	142
Mill and market	208
Missionary	25
Mohammed	184
Momentum	128
Moody, D. L.	246
Moral distinctions	254
Morality and religion	19
Mozley, Canon	22
Murray, Andrew	157, 159
Napoleon	130
Nations	236
Nature, study of	200
Nehemiah	206
New Jerusalem	18
Newton, John	82
Newton, Sir Isaac	132
New wine	6
Office, prostituting public	252
Organization, power of	273
Overcoming life	207
Palace Beautiful	260
Parables, Dives and Lazarus	56
—— Man on island	281
—— Rich farmer	57
—— Unjust steward	293
Parker, Theo	165
Parkhurst, C. H.	122
Pascal	49
Patience	162, 163

	PAGE
Patriotism	249
Paul, quoted	70, 73, 86, 179, 180
Perfection	16
Persecuted	150
Peter, apostle	280
Pharisees	33, 193
Phelps, Austin	195
Pilate, Pontius	89
—— and Christ	243
Pilgrim's calling	17
Plato	29, 211, 239
Pleasure	190
Politics	250
—— "Sunday school"	257
Politician, on being	244
Political consciousness	238
Pope Boniface VIII	12
Pompilia	203
Prayer	95
—— Christian	118
—— Elements of	106
—— Habit of	136
—— Kinds of	111
—— Lord's prayer	110, 116, 118
—— Natural	116
—— Selfish	114
—— Objections to	102
—— Reasons for	96
Pride	158
Progress	41
Protestantism	14
Puritans	71, 191
Race, unity of	15
Reading habit	140
Reconciliation	83
Recreation	193
Redeemed world	178
Reformation	13
Religion and morality	19
—— False views of	28
Revelation, how given	7
Richter, Jean Paul	99
Righteousness	19
Right ideals	30
Robertson, F. W.	98, 176
Roman world	10
Rosetta stone	50
Rothe	6
Royal law	228
Ruskin, John	21, 30, 49, 160, 162, 185, 226
Sacred and secular	174
Sacrifice	87
Sacrificial life	90
Sainthood, traditional	21
Salvation	20, 167
Saxons	147

INDEX.

	PAGE
Scriptures, a revelation	51
—— Profitable	72
Second century life	8
Seeley, J. R.	235
Sermon on Mount	148
Service, mutual	27
Shaftesbury, Earl of	49
Shakespeare,	38, 112
Sin	80
—— deliverance from	79
Slavery	211
Smith, Geo. Adam	144
Solidarity	16, 237
Sonship	103
Speculation	225
Spirit, ruling	154
Spirituality	183
Standards	60
Stalker, James	153
State	237
—— Ideals for	247
—— Jewish	242
—— Necessary to man	242
—— A partnership	240
Steward, unjust	203
Stewards, faithful	299
St. Francis	185
Table made by Christ	179
Tennyson	43, 55, 98, 106, 256, 296
Thackeray	96
Thankfulness	106
Time saved	142
Tolstoi, Leo	151, 240
Trade	209
Trader	217
Transformed life	46

	PAGE
Truth	89
Twelve apostles, teaching of	8
Types	50
Vanity Fair	188
Vanity of vanities	37
Virtue	19
—— Habitual	134
Virtues	20
—— Efficiency of passive	152
—— Ideals of	146
—— Passive	146
Visions and ideals	29
Wagner, Charles	188, 190, 213
Ward, Lester F.	222, 231
Wellington, Duke of	130
Westcott, Bishop B. F.	208, 235, 236
Whittier	144
Williams, W. R.	162
Woman of Samaria	170
Work	210
—— Despised	211
—— Honest	201
—— Necessary	210
—— Scamped	181
—— Service in	218
—— Significance of	214
Worship	106
—— Promoted	268
White, Kirke	37
Youth, time of visions	85
Zechariah	173

www.ingramcontent.com/pod-product-compliance
Lightning Source LLC
Chambersburg PA
CBHW022049230426
43672CB00008B/1122